THE WAYSIDE GARDENS COLLECTION

The
SHADY GARDEN

THE WAYSIDE GARDENS COLLECTION

The
SHADY
GARDEN

A Practical Guide to Planning & Planting

Jane Taylor

John E. Elsley, General Editor for The Wayside Gardens Collection

 **Sterling Publishing Co., Inc. New York**

Library of Congress Cataloging-in-Publication Data Available

2 4 6 8 10 9 7 5 3 1

Published 1994 by Sterling Publishing Company, Inc.
387 Park Avenue South, New York, N.Y. 10016
The Wayside Gardens Collection edition

American Project Editor	Hannah Steinmetz
Project Editor	Jane O'Shea
Project Art Editor	Ann Burnham
Editors	Barbara Mellor
	Caroline Davison
Picture Researcher	Jessica Walton
Production	Julia Golding
Illustrators	Shirley Felts
	Gilly Newman
	Valerie Alford
	Pauline Dean

Sterling ISBN 0-8069-0841-6

FRONT JACKET Helleborus orientalis.
BACK JACKET Saxifraga × urbium *(left),* Dryopteris
(right) against Acer palmatum *var.* dissectum
'Dissectum Atropurpureum.'
PAGE 1 Hosta fortunei *var.* albopicta *(left), pansies
and* H. sieboldiana *var.* elegans *(right).*
PAGE 2 Tulipa sprengeri *(left),* Rodgersia
podophyllum *(right) and* Helleborus orientalis
(foreground right).
RIGHT *Tender ferns beneath a tree canopy, with
mauve-and-white* Acanthus *spikes and a clump of
black-leaved* Ophiopogon planiscapus nigrescens.

CONTENTS

IN THRALL TO SHADE GARDENING

To some gardeners, the idea of growing things in shade can be rather daunting. Their only experience of shady places may have been the dense, difficult shade beneath an overbearing tree, where periwinkle may be the only thing growing. This book aims to show you how rewarding shade gardening can be; what a range of plants there are that are endowed with elegance, charm, fine or dramatic lines—qualities that endure when the jazzy charms of border flowers have palled.

This group exemplifies much of what is best in shade gardening: cool, fresh harmonies, beautiful foliage, and flowers that demand to be examined closely. The shuttlecocks of the ostrich plume fern (Matteuccia struthiopteris) form a curving sweep around the divided, jagged leaves of Astrantia major, its green-white pincushion flowers floating above the fern and the lime-green froth of Alchemilla mollis.

Of course, some kinds of shade can present real problems. Some of these are discussed, with ideas for solutions, in the next chapter. It is no coincidence, however, that "problem shade" takes up just part of the chapter, while the rest of the book is about the tremendous opportunities that shade presents.

Perhaps, like me, you have memories of the dappled shade of a romantic, overgrown garden; I remember with particular nostalgia the coolness beneath a cherry tree. When I began to garden for myself, I knew little about the plants that would thrive in that welcome shade—honesty and ferns were all I could recall. Trying to learn enough to make a passable garden, I read all the gardening books I could find, and visited other people's gardens. It was through these visits, above all, that I became aware of the great range of plants that grew well in shade, even in gray-skied Britain. When, after a few years, I found myself with an almost bare two acres, I realized that the contours of the site gave me a choice of sun and ready-made shade, and that nature's hand had thoughtfully disposed a few silver birches and ragged hawthorns on the banks to vary the patterns of light and shadow.

RIGHT *The pink lockets of* Dicentra formosa *are set off by its blue-green, dissected foliage, contrasting with hellebore foliage and the soft-textured, golden-green blades and airy citron sprays of Mr. Bowles' golden grass,* Milium effusum aureum, *in a relaxed, close-mingled planting typical of the shady garden.*

OPPOSITE *A bough of* Cornus kousa, *laden with creamy bracts, arches over an azalea in this idyllic woodland setting. Two energetic ground-covering perennials,* Lamium galeobdolon *'Florentinum' with its silver-splashed leaves, and the woodruff,* Galium odoratum *(syn.* Asperula odorata), *carpet the leafy soil.*

RIGHT *Fritillaria pallidiflora is one of the best species for the shady garden, easy to grow in rich, leafy soil in light or dappled shade.*

RIGHT *The subtle tinting of the young foliage of Epimedium grandiflorum is enhanced by the tiny white hairs fringing the leaves, and the long-spurred white flowers seem to be poised in flight on their wiry stems.*

The site had its problems, not least the lack of topsoil, but it also had enormous potential. There was a stream, big sweeping banks facing away from the sun for bold foliage effects, one high shady wall by a waterfall, and sandstone to build retaining walls–almost instant scope for planting small, special treasures. In the pages that follow I describe how I improved the terrible soil, and share with you how I coped with dense dry shade.

I soon began to recall those visits to other gardens, the restful sweeps of hostas and lady's mantle (*Alchemilla mollis*), the fleeting peony flowers and the dainty lockets of bleeding heart (*Dicentra spectabilis*). I still knew little about the small-scale plants of the shady garden that demand to be scrutinized at close quarters: but I was on my way to being a shade gardener.

In this book I have chosen for you the best shade-loving plants, given you practical tips on growing them, and suggested ideas for combining them to best effect. Above all, I have tried to stress the joy of gardening in shade, and to convey to you the special qualities of the plants that love shady places.

For there is, of course, absolutely no substitute for growing plants for yourself. You will not really be in thrall to shade gardening until you have run your fingers through the stiff, metallic fronds of a holly fern and contrasted their texture with the soft lace of a polystichum, peered into the intricate, speckled heart of a toad lily or been provoked to laughter by the absurd little mouse plant, marveled at the poise of a trout lily or been stirred nostalgically by the old-fashioned charm of a double primrose.

As well as these small delights, shade gardening has grander effects to capture your heart. The purpose of making a garden, it has been said, is to paint beautiful pictures with plants. In a shady garden, to the beauty of the plants themselves is added the play of light and shade, ever-changing with the march of the sun, the passage of the seasons, and the movement of the wind. Once this kind of gardening is in your soul, you will never wish for a garden without shade again.

LEFT *A study in contrasts of foliage and form in this half-shaded border, where in the foreground* Hosta sieboldiana *is set beside a crested fern; beyond, more hostas, ferns and* Alchemilla mollis *with a white lacecap hydrangea in bud. The creamy flowers of* Phygelius 'Yellow Trumpet' *are outlined against the wall, across the path from the blades of day lilies* (Hemerocallis). Lilium regale *brings touches of white, and its powerful perfume, to the border.*

LEFT *A spring cameo with* Corydalis lutea *and forget-me-nots (left), and (right) the bright magenta-rose pea flowers of* Lathyrus vernus. *The soft shield fern (*Polystichum setiferum*) behind is not at its best in spring but will come into its own as these spring flowers fade and its new fronds unfurl.*

HOW MUCH SHADE?

Shade in the garden is not a matter of either/or, of sun or shadow: there are many different qualities of shade, and no scientific way of measuring their effect on plants. Nursery catalogs, if they give any guidance at all, tend to make it all too simple, with only three categories: full shade, half shade, or sun. To get the most from a shady garden, and to assess its possibilities or potential problems, you need to be able to identify with accuracy the nature of your shade.

Among the joys of a shady garden are the play of sun and shadow on the plants, changing with the seasons and moving with the wind. Here, the darkly glowing blue lanterns of Clematis alpina *are set among the white, gold-flecked flowers of an azalea, reflecting every ray of light.*

Types of shade

BELOW *House walls can provide a variety of environments, one of the most friendly to plants being shade for half the day. Ferns, hostas and* Euphorbia wulfenii *are among the shade-tolerant foliage plants in the border here that are enlivened in their season by the flowers of lilies and white valerian. Flowering climbers, a white rose and the pineapple broom,* Cytisus battandieri, *take advantage of the extra warmth that is provided by the walls.*

There are in fact not just two but at least three basic types of shade: full, half and dappled shade. Each varies with the nature and height of existing planting and of surrounding walls and buildings. Wind and humidity play an important part, too, as does the nature of your soil.

Full shade

This comes in at least three basic forms: the friendly shadow to the sunless side of a hedge, wall or building; the cold, dank shade of places where neither sunlight nor air brings relief; and the dense shade beneath a thick-canopied tree. This may last all year round, as under a mature hemlock or evergreen oak, or throughout the summer, as under a beech or sycamore maple. Places beneath steps and balconies can be very difficult. Here, as under light-blocking trees, it may be too dark and also too dry to grow anything permanently.

Half shade

Half shade implies sun for about half of the day; it makes quite a difference to plants whether this is morning or afternoon sun, or intermittent sun and shade during the whole of the day. Morning shade followed by afternoon sun is hard on shade-loving plants, which can all too easily bake during a hot afternoon when the sun's rays are stronger and the humidity lower; afternoon shade is kinder, and intermittent shadow generally helpful to plants.

The source of the shade may be a wall, fence or building, or the slanting shadow of a tree canopy. Plants in the shadow of a wall have to cope with the extra warmth retained by the brick or stone: this can be a problem for shade plants, especially as the soil at the foot of a wall is commonly rather dry. Half shade from trees is generally preferable, unless you can keep the humidity up, in which case you have one of the finest garden habitats: winter-warm shade.

RIGHT *An old fruit tree provides kindly dappled shade for the plants that grow beneath its branches. A mixture of pink and white Spanish bluebells (*Hyacinthoides hispanica*) have pushed their way through pink-flowered heaths and a prostrate cotoneaster. Grown in a bed retained by a low stone wall, their soft tones add lightness to the rugged tree bark and somber gray path.*

Light or dappled shade

The most desirable of all types of shade may be the light shade cast by high-branching deciduous trees, or the dappled shade beneath those with an open branch structure and small leaves. The chief danger with high-branching trees is that blocks of sunlight may fall across shade-loving plants when the sun is at its highest; tender foliage can scorch all too quickly on hot days. Many plants also thrive in the open-sky shadow of a low wall or building, or of distant trees or buildings, especially if the shadow falls during the hottest hours in the middle of the day.

Remember, too, that levels of atmospheric humidity affect plants' response to light and shadow: the more moisture in the air, the more sun a shade-loving plant will stand. The thief of humidity is wind; so if your garden is exposed, you will need more shade for your woodland treasures than a neighbor who shelters behind trees and hedges.

Evidently, if you live in an area where the days are usually bright and sunny and the rainfall is low, your plants will need more shade than if your climate is cloudy, cool and wet. In hot, bright climates, light or dappled shade is virtually the same, from the plants' point of view, as full sun.

The composition of your soil will also affect the performance of shade-loving plants. Most do best in a neutral or mildly acid soil; some, notably virtually every member of the great Ericaceae family, need a decidedly acid soil. A pH of 5.5 and below will enable you to grow rhododendrons and azaleas. If you are making your shade garden among existing trees, you should be able to guess the soil type by looking at the trees in your plot. Elm, ash and black locust are generally found on alkaline soils. Under oaks, mountain ash, some maples, birch and conifers the soil is generally acid. Established conifers also cast a dense shade unless many of their lower branches are removed, as do certain evergreen broad-leaved trees such as evergreen oak. On pages 24–6 you will find tips for improving the soil; ideal shade garden soil such as you might find under a stand of mature oaks, for example, is rare.

Easy shade

Gardeners who want to grow the widest range of shade-loving plants will contrive to create areas of dappled sunlight and shadow, areas where the soil is cool and the atmosphere ever moist, and sheltered places for warm shade. They will devise sheltered areas, using temporary screens, both living and artificial, and they will know that even one or two garden trees can suggest a copse or pocket of woodland if the soil, canopy and shelter are right.

While waiting for their trees to grow, they will seize every advantage, even the small shadow of a

rock or shrub, to make homes for shade plants. They may borrow ideas from tropical gardens and build a lath house to shelter shade plants in beds or pots (see page 96). I know many houses in Karachi, a desert city, where lath houses make a delightful extension of the dwelling house, a place to sit among ferns and luxuriant foliage on hot summer days.

Even if your garden does not lend itself to a permanent structure such as a lath house, you can devise temporary shading for your plants using a variety of materials, from picket, board or bamboo fencing to brand-name wind- and sun-screen materials woven from plastic. In this way, you will be able

FAR LEFT *A planting of deciduous purple hazels (*Corylus maxima *'Purpurea') provides a light summer canopy for wild flowers—yellow Welsh poppy (*Meconopsis cambrica*), ferns and cow parsley, also known as Queen Anne's lace. The naturalistic planting contrasts with the square paving slabs laid diamond-wise.*

LEFT *The lacy fronds of ferns and the broad blades of hostas, both green- and white-variegated (*H. ventricosa *and* H. *'Thomas Hogg'), are complemented by the bold leaves of* Hydrangea quercifolia *and the grace of bamboos. Moss and mind-your-own-business (*Soleirolia soleirolii*) cover the soil at their feet to the exclusion of weeds.*

to grow quite a range of shade plants, even in a new and open garden. The shade cast by an artificial screen is different, it is true, from that of a tree canopy; there is none of the play of light and shadow, simply a pool of shade for part of the day. But against that, your shade-loving plants will have the chance to establish themselves without having to contend with competition from the roots of an already mature tree.

To make shade in the early years, fast-growing shrubs such as spiraeas and buddlejas can be used among the slower, more permanent shrubs of your framework (see the chapter on the framework on page 29). By their nature, though, they risk encroaching on slower or smaller plants: you must be prepared to be firm, even ruthless, with the pruning shears, and to treat these quick-growing shrubs as a short-term measure, grubbing them out as the permanent framework of shrubs and trees begins to fill out and provide an overhead canopy.

Given this variety of habitats—and it is remarkable what can be achieved even in a very small garden—the jazzy charms of conventional flower borders and bedding schemes soon lose their allure in the face of the lovely leaves and the intriguing, subtle beauty of woodland flowers.

ABOVE *In this spare, formal courtyard of clipped box and raked gravel, with a path of tiles set on edge for easy walking, incidents—a hydrangea in a tub, a plant of* Euphorbia wulfenii—*are less important than the play of light and the shade of standard trees, so welcome in a hot climate.*

Problem shade

If you are starting from scratch, you can aim for the ideal mix of shade and habitats. Unfortunately, just as life is never perfect, so gardens often fall short of the ideal. The shade you already have may represent more of a problem than an opportunity; or, to be more optimistic, you may have to use some ingenuity to realize its potential. Look for the good points: maybe your tree has good bark or dramatic buttresses at the base of the trunk. If so, it could become a feature, with the planting to the periphery, where there will be more light. If you do decide to plant, you will find the most challenging areas are in dense, dry, rooty shade; and in cold, dank or drafty shade.

The minimalist solution to the permanent dark shade cast by evergreen trees, or by heavy-canopied deciduous trees too large to have their lower branches lopped, could be to spread chipped bark or light-colored, coarse sand thickly beneath the tree. Pick or rake fallen leaves away in their season, and enjoy the tree without any visual distractions. If this is too stark for you, the extra light reflected by pale sand may be enough to grow plants in containers, at least temporarily. Remove them to convalescent quarters as soon as they show signs of needing more light, and remember that the tree canopy will keep rain from them as effectively as from the soil below.

The optimist, determined to grow plants even in the most unpropitious conditions, may view this as defeatist. Beneath a deciduous tree that lets in light and rain during the winter months, but casts a heavy shade when in leaf, the planting options are wider.

Before attempting to plant under a tree, try the soil with a spade to see how rooty it is. The toughest shade plants will cope even if you simply dig holes between the main roots of your tree and plant them with ideal shade soil, rich in organic matter (see page 26). Try to avoid hacking through large roots, though if you do damage the odd one, inadvertently or in desperation, probably no great harm will result. You will need to see that your underplantings are watered thoroughly, kept moist during the dry months, and given a yearly feed in spring.

Plants that should do well with this treatment include the Irish ivy, *Hedera hibernica* (a ground-spreader with huge leaves, not a climber), the evergreen spurge, *Euphorbia amygdaloides* var. *robbiae*, periwinkles (*Vinca*) and, in acid soils, *Pachysandra terminalis* and the salal, *Gaultheria shallon*. To encourage dense growth, cut out the flowering stems of the spurge once they are over.

Drought-tolerant ferns likely to be able to cope with rooty shade include the male fern *Dryopteris filix-mas*, the hard fern *Blechnum spicant*, and *Polypodium vulgare*. The polypody and the hard fern are also evergreen except where frosts are very severe.

RIGHT *In this small courtyard the shadow of a tall eucalyptus, and its greedy root system, restrict the choice of plants. Sword ferns and two tree ferns indicate a mild climate; a dark-leaved ivy covers the ground and runs tentative arms up the eucalyptus trunk. Only where more light enters can the roses and flowering plants be grown. The soil has been top-dressed with a leafy mixture to nourish the ferns and ivy.*

Planting beneath a large tree

If the soil is too rooty to dig, spread a blend of leafy, loose soil (see page 26) over the roots, away from the trunk. You will need at least 6–8in in depth, and you will need to water during the summer, whatever you plant. It is also worth adding fertilizer each spring and keeping the ground mulched with organic matter, preferably the kind with nutrients in it rather than sterile peat or bark. The tree will take much of what you offer, but your shade plants will use the leftovers and do much better as a result.

This group looks well in winter when, left to right, Helleborus foetidus *is in flower, the elegant evergreen foliage of* Danae racemosa *comes into its own,* Iris foetidissima *bears its showy seeds and the* Polypodium vulgare *and* Cyclamen hederifolium *are in leaf.*

PLANTING BENEATH A TREE

Plants with firm evergreen foliage

Danae racemosa: arching stems and glossy narrow leaves.

Daphne odora: gleaming foliage, fragrant creamy-white flowers in spring.

Helleborus foetidus: spires of green flowers in winter.

Iris foetidissima: spear leaves, orange seeds in fall/winter.

Ferns

Dryopteris filix-mas (male fern): tough and easygoing.

Polypodium vulgare (polypody): tolerant of drought but more luxuriant if watered.

Polystichum setiferum (soft shield fern): sensitive to spring drought.

Bulbous and carpeting plants

Cyclamen hederifolium: grows right up to tree trunks, pink or white flowers in the fall.

Eranthis hyemalis: (winter aconite): yellow flowers in early spring.

Omphalodes cappadocica: blue forget-me-not flowers in spring.

19

Dank, drafty shade

This is probably an even greater challenge than the shadow beneath a domineering tree. Cutting winds are often worst in winter and early spring, making all but the toughest evergreens vulnerable. Once they have shed their leaves, deciduous shrubs do little to sift the wind at its coldest; and if you choose them for their flowers they will not perform as well in these dark places as they would in better light.

Here again there is the minimalist (some might say defeatist) solution of no plants, just sand, pebbles or paving. Think about a no-plants treatment, and it might, paradoxically, suggest ways of making the place less hostile to plant life. Can you bring in reflected light with mirrors or a whitewashed wall, perhaps, or even just by choosing the palest surfaces of paving or sand? Can you contrive to sift the cold winds without losing still more light?

In acid soil, try the toughest hardy hybrid rhododendrons: *Rhododendron* 'Scintillation' in light pink, 'Nova-Zembla' in bright-red, or 'Cunningham's White.' *R.* 'P.J.M.' or its hybrids can be welcome where little else will grow. If you hate its lavender-pink color, try *R. catawbiense* in lilac to white. Low, fast-spreading *Gaultheria shallon* grows in the deepest shade, though you should not expect much flower from it in dark places. A more elegant and better-behaved choice, *Leucothoë fontanesiana* also does quite well in deep shade.

Any soil suits the indomitable *Lonicera pileata* and the Oregon grape, *Mahonia aquifolium*. The butcher's broom, *Ruscus aculeatus*, is less graceful than the related *Danae*, but correspondingly easier-going, and prickly enough to deter invaders. *Viburnum davidii* has bold, deeply veined, glossy green leaves and makes good ground-cover, as do ivy and periwinkles (*Vinca major* and the smaller, neater *V. minor*), as well as the creeping *Euonymus fortunei*, which climbs given the support of a wall or tree trunk.

Deciduous shrubs such as dogwoods (*Cornus alba* and *C. stolonifera*), *Kerria japonica*, *Viburnum opulus*, the Guelder rose, and its sterile "snowball" cultivar 'Roseum' (which is white), and even the cultivars of *Hydrangea paniculata* are tough and resistant to cold. Do all you can to improve the soil and they should forgive you the cold and the lack of light.

Non-woody perennials add to the range of possibilities. Many bergenias cope with the most unpropitious conditions and their bold, evergreen leaves look well with paving or stones. The off-white daisies of *Tanacetum macrophyllum* (syn. *Chrysanthemum macrophyllum*) lack quality, but this is a very forgiving tall, summer-flowering perennial. With a little more light, *Campanula latifolia* should cope too, producing steeples of lilac or white bells in summer. If toughies like these thrive, be adventurous; you never know what you may get away with.

TOOLS FOR PRUNING

- You will need high-quality scissor-action hand pruners, a folding handsaw, a pair of long-handled cutters and a plastic or canvas sheet to collect the prunings.
- For branches too high to reach with the saw or hand pruners, you will need steps or a ladder; you might also find a pole saw useful, or hand pruners on a pole, operated with a pull-cord (fiddly to use).
- Twigs can be cut cleanly with sharp hand pruners; branchlets with the saw. With thicker branches, you will need to start by sawing the underside of the branch, to avoid tearing the bark as the branch falls.

Opening out cluttered branches

The first step in creative pruning is to contemplate the tree, to decide what you want to achieve. With reasonably mature trees, the most likely reasons for pruning are to reduce the clutter of too many branchlets and crossing branches, or to remove branches that are too low (limbing up). Pruning young trees is dealt with on pages 38–9.

The work may be done in summer, when the tree is in leaf; or in winter, when you will need to exercize all your imagination and memory to envisage the results next summer.

The branch before pruning: branchlets and twigs to be removed are marked, and a crossing pair identified.

Twiggy growth, one of the crossing branches and a branch growing inwards have been removed.

The end result: a tree with fewer and stouter branches, such as Magnolia × soulangeana, could look even sparer.

LEFT *Even dark and drafty shade is not too challenging for tough perennials such as bergenias, hart's tongue fern (*Phyllitis scolopendrium*) and acanthus, which combine here to make a pattern of contrasting leaf form and shades of green in this planting at the foot of a stone ornament.*

Arborizing a shrub

Large shrubs can sometimes be made into trees with a single stem, or perhaps two or three, springing from ground level. Examine all your large shrubs to see if there is a tree inside waiting to be liberated. If so, you will gain a patch of ground ready for planting with shade treasures. Lilacs, laurels, some viburnums and maybe even a rhododendron or a juniper could be treated in this way.

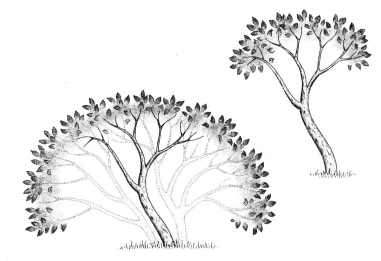

Aim to retain a spreading canopy of branches above the trunks, and cut away unwanted branches at ground level or flush with the trunk so there are no stubs to spoil the outline.

The maturing of a shady garden

English bluebells (Hyacinthoides non-scripta) have carpeted the ground beneath an avenue of lindens, with just a narrow, foot-trodden path drawing a line across the blue sward. Because they increase and spread fast, they are not ideal bulbs for small gardens.

However much you enhance and control the growth and the branching of your trees and shrubs, you cannot halt the process of maturing, only guide it. In nature the woodland canopy thickens with the years, casting ever-denser shade; then comes the final stage, senescence and decay. Trees, like people, have their natural span: flowering cherries fall into decrepitude within the lifetime of a gardener, oaks will long outlive those who plant them.

If you are obliged to move house frequently this process may not concern you, but you may one day move into a house with a mature garden around it. And those who stay put for even a decade or two are amazed at the speed with which the new garden takes on first an established, then a mature aspect.

Be prepared, then, as time passes, to revise your shade plantings; to move individual plants as the shadow cast upon them becomes more than they enjoy, or—with the felling of a tree or fall of a branch—less than they need. Few decisions are irrevocable in the garden; few plants, and this is especially true of those of the forest floor, cannot be moved successfully even when established.

In the managed environment of a garden, where to some extent you can control levels of shade, you can choose your underplantings to suit your taste and conditions. In nature, as the years pass and the woodland canopy grows denser, flowering plants beneath yield to ferns, and ultimately to a carpet of mosses alone.

ABOVE *A green carpet of moss shows off to perfection the white flowers of the wood anemone (Anemone nemorosa) and the clean bole of the tree, itself just greened at the base with moss. Distant shrubs offer no distraction from the restful simplicity.*

Using moss and ferns

In places too dark for flowering plants, yet moist enough to support plant life, mosses and ferns may thrive. They are beautiful in their own right, and will also enhance the uncluttered trunks of trees rising above them.

Encourage moss and discourage weeds by applying spot applications of Roundup® to actively growing foliage, following the manufacturer's instructions. The chemical destroys all green things (remember to keep it clear of ferns).

The chapter on key plants (see page 107) gives a selection of the finest ferns. Those which form single crowns, such as *Polystichum setiferum*, should be kept uncluttered: remove secondary crowns as they develop. Others, such as the oak fern (*Gymnocarpium dryopteris*) and beech fern (*Phegopteris connectilis*), are frail and airy, with running roots forming colonies.

At the lighter margins you could allow the occasional clump of early-flowering woodlanders that retire quickly below ground, such as clintonias, wood anemones, or small bulbs.

Creating or improving the soil

Polystichum setiferum

In Victorian times fern collecting was a craze, and aberrant forms found in the wild would be dug up (something that would be quite unacceptable in these conservation-conscious days) to be planted in a pteridophile's fernery. This fern is sedate compared with the bizarrely crested variants of fern, some more like needleworker's braid than any living plant.

Tough shade plants such as bergenias, spotted laurels (*Aucuba*) and *Iris foetidissima* will grow in almost any soil, and many more will do in reasonable soil with extra organic matter. But many shade-loving plants are woodlanders by nature, and do best in a woodland soil. Your shade gardening will be far more rewarding if you create the right loose, moist, leafy medium for your plants to grow in.

In a brand-new plot, as yet ungardened, you may find anything from reasonable topsoil spread by the builders (but hiding who knows what horrors, such as rubble or cement spills) to bare subsoil. The soil in established gardens, with or without existing shade, could be fast-draining, hungry sand, sticky clay lying wet in winter and baking to a hard creviced texture in summer, or, with great luck, a workable, well-nourished and well-drained loam. All these can be made into a suitable medium for shade plants.

When starting from totally unsuitable subsoil, at least you know where you stand. If it is workable, break it up, with a pick if need be; if not, you can build up soil on top of it. You will have to create the planting medium for yourself. I have done this on a base of coal-mine waste, shale and rock, and within three years—without great expense—made 6in of fluffy topsoil in which I could plant with a trowel, or even

fingers. And this was a plot measuring approximately 2 acres, much of it situated on steepish slopes. It was achieved mainly by mulching with any available organic matter—garden compost, peat moss and leaf mold collected from the neighboring woods, ground bark, sawdust from the nearby sawmill, farmyard manure (bartered for jelly and vegetables), coconut fiber, spent mushroom compost, spent hops, even once-used potting soil.

The possibilities are many, and you too may be able to find sources of cheap or free-for-the-taking organic matter to build up a fair depth of future shade soil. Even in a new garden, it is surprising how quickly you can accumulate enough weeds and lawn clippings to form a compost heap, supplementing it with vegetable waste, carpet sweepings and so on from the house, and even small quantities of shredded newspaper.

Well-made compost should become hot enough to kill weed seeds, but if you have any doubts, instead of using the compost as a mulch (which could simply make your weed problem worse instead of helping to solve it) you could use it in planting holes only, so that it is never actually on the surface. If you have two compost bays, you can have one heap in the making and one ready to use at all times.

Making garden compost

A compost heap will quickly turn weeds and so forth into dark, crumbly nutrients for your plants. For small gardens the plastic bins you can buy ready-made are satisfactory, but you could construct a special compost corner in an out-of-the-way place. The quicker you build up your heap, the hotter it should become. Keep it covered with sacking or strips of old carpet, to keep the heat in and the rain out. After a while, turn the heap sides to middle, so unrotted material from the outside can heat up and rot in turn.

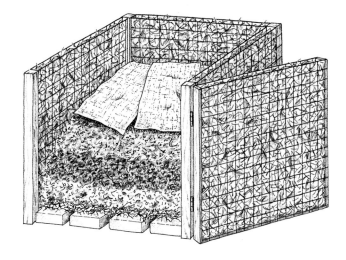

Use boards, or a wire netting sandwich padded with straw, to make an open-topped, solid-sided area for your compost; one side can be open. Lay some bricks on the base for ventilation, and cover them with a layer of coarse material or woody, twiggy prunings.

Build layers of weeds, herbaceous tops, vegetable household waste, and lawn mowings mixed with coarser material. After each 6in layer, sprinkle on some organic fertilizer or brand-name compost accelerator. Add a sprinkling of woodfire ash from time to time; ash contains potash.

ABOVE *An unexpected fall vignette, where the crisp golden-brown fallen leaves of a beech hedge lie among and on the bold, leathery foliage of bergenias and on the path alongside. Beech leaves are among the best for mulching woodland soil, rotting to a flaky, crumbly-textured, rich brown leaf mold. If a heavier carpet fell on the bergenia, it would need to be cleared.*

Creating ideal soil for shade plants

BELOW *A woodland planting in late spring is bright with the spires of bugle* (Ajuga pyramidalis), *the milky spires of the foam flower* (Tiarella cordifolia), *and lilac-pink forget-me-nots. Hostas and the arching stems of* Smilacina racemosa *add form to the sweeps of color.*

You need ample quantities of organic matter–leaf mold, well-rotted compost, peat moss, even spent mushroom compost if you do not intend to grow lime-haters. Add grit or coarse sand to open the mixture, and some loamy soil to add body. If any of the proposed components contain rocks, roots or clods, it is worth sifting them through a coarse screen. The ideal proportions are: two parts organic matter, one part sand or grit, one part loam. If you want to grow the kind of special plants described in the chapter on cameos and collectibles (see page 83), you will need to aim for this ideal, which will be light, fluffy, free-draining and moisture-retentive.

All but the most exacting of shade plants will do well enough, however, if there is twice or three times as much sand or many times more organic matter. In my own coal-pit garden I used neat organic matter, mainly leaf mold and garden compost; the worms soon mixed it with the shale and the result suited my woodland plants very well. If both the grit and the loam are neutral to acid in reaction, and your natural soil also, you will be able to grow just about any shade plant successfully.

The mixture you create can be used in many ways. It can be used to improve existing soil, to spread over impossible subsoil or root-filled areas, in raised beds, in containers, or on concrete (retain the mixture with railroad ties, boards, tree branches or thinnish trunks, even concrete blocks if you have no alternative).

Turning a lawn into soil

If you want to turn lawn or grassland into ideal shade-garden soil, there are several ways to go about it. Mow the grass first, and mark off the areas you want to keep as lawn. You can then deal with the grass you do not want by weed-killing it with a biodegradable contact herbicide; by stripping the turf (stack it to use as loam in the future); by digging the grass in (thick grass will come up again; very sparse growth should be killed by turning in); or by killing it by excluding light.

One way to do this is to split straw bales into slabs about 2in thick, and lay them over the area to be killed out, making sure they overlap so no light gets through. (This has even been known to banish quack grass, but you will need to cover the whole area of quack for this to work.) By the time the straw has begun to rot down (making extra organic matter for the soil) the grass should be dead. Another method, untried by me but recommended by a talented American shade gardener, George Schenk, is to spread newspapers over the area, ten sheets or more thick, and either spread a thin layer of soil over the top or, more extravagantly, a 6–8in layer. In the latter case you will be able to plant immediately; otherwise you should wait six months or so for the grass to die out. Meanwhile, weeds are likely to find your nice new soil a tempting habitat.

Maintaining the shady garden

Successful maintenance involves both cosmetic work and ensuring your plants remain healthy and productive. In woodland soil fertilizer is seldom essential for healthy growth, but applying a well-balanced fertilizer in early spring wherever the soil is less than ideal (annually where it is very poor, otherwise less frequently) should result in stronger growth, lusher leaves and more flowers.

Annual mulching is even more important: it not only conserves moisture, but also helps to maintain soil in the desirable loose, leafy texture beloved by shade plants. Nature's way is to mulch in the fall, with the annual leaf fall, but in the garden a controlling hand is needed. Very small plants can be smothered by fallen leaves and should be cleared before winter's wet finishes them off, but larger ones benefit from the leafy blanket. Ardent woodland gardeners whose tree canopy is still inadequate to provide enough leaves obtain extra supplies and add them among shrubs and larger perennials. The best leaves, most woodland gardeners agree, are beech or oak, because they rot down quite quickly to a dry, flaky mixture. However, if your natural soil is acid and you want to grow lime-hating plants, or if you have made a special bed of acid soil so you can grow them even if your natural soil is limy, remember that beechwoods are often found in alkaline soil, and oaks may be, and that according to some the leaves from any tree growing on alkaline or lime soil will produce alkaline leaf mold.

If the leaves you propose to use as a mulch are damp, you can ensure they stay put in all but the most exposed gardens by taking them in firm double handfuls and packing them closely among your shrubs. The layer of leaves should be as much as 5in deep among shrubs and trees–be sure, though, that the area immediately around the collar of trees and shrub stems is kept clear in order to avoid collar rot. Among smaller plants, carpeting shrubs and others which would be choked by a thick leaf layer, it is better to apply a mulch of finely ground bark or well-rotted leaf mold. The best time to do this is in late spring or in early summer.

If you cannot obtain leaves in quantities large enough to be worth using as a mulch, you can use well-rotted garden compost, ground bark or most of the other sources of organic matter already mentioned. The least satisfactory of these is peat: apart from the environmental concerns about despoiling peat bogs, it all too easily dries out and blows away, and if you use a layer thick enough to make a worthwhile mulch it is ruinously expensive.

A generous mulch also helps to protect the roots of your plants against frost. After frosty spells, go round the garden firming in anything that has been heaved up by the frost, or the roots will quickly dry out. During dry spells in the growing season, be prepared to water. As in the open garden, infrequent but generous, deep-reaching irrigation is far better for plants than frequent sprinklings.

ABOVE *A fall mulch of leaves mixed with small twigs lasts the winter through to retain both warmth and moisture in the soil. In summer it will help to keep weeds at bay too, and as it rots it will nourish the soil. But a mulch is not just for utility. Even without the vivid daffodils this would be a beautiful picture, the cosy mulch setting off the bare trunks and the graceful branches of a multi-stemmed tree.*

THE FRAMEWORK

Any garden is better for a firm design, in which the right balance is struck between the framework—trees, hedges, path and lawn, and the permanent, often evergreen, elements of planting—and the planting spaces. Here I want to consider the plantings that form part of the framework of the garden. Important everywhere, in the shady garden they are essential, for to a large degree they create the shade that gives the garden its character.

Beneath the arching branches of trees, this shady garden has a firm framework of enduring foliage and a unifying ground-planting. Ivy-clad walls add to the sense of a green enclosure, and make a textured backdrop to the bold foliage of a mahonia (left), the leathery paddles of bergenias (right) and the upstanding spears of iris leaves on either side of the paved path.

Shade-giving trees

Trees vary greatly as shade-givers. Some are friendly, both at the root and overhead; others are greedy and overbearing. If you move into a garden where the trees are already mature you will have to make the best of them; if you are starting from a bare site, it makes sense to choose the trees that best combine beauty with usefulness as shade-givers.

While it is natural to want quick results from your plantings, it is not necessarily productive to spend a fortune on lots of extra-heavy standard trees (the trade term for trees grown on a tall stem to a large size in the nursery). It could nevertheless be worth investing in just one such tree, provided the right kind is available, to give at least the illusion of a quick start as well as a small area of instant canopy.

In the long term, however, the best results come from planting small. The younger your tree, within reason, the better able it will be to establish itself as the roots take hold in its new surroundings. A young container-grown tree should be well rooted but not pot-bound; if the roots have grown out through the drainage holes or the pot is so filled with roots that they are curling round each other, the tree may never become firmly rooted. If you buy bare-rooted or balled and burlapped trees, ensure the roots have not been damaged in the lifting; the ideal nursery-grown

tree will have been undercut or lifted more than once while growing on, so as to form a ball of fibrous roots which will suffer little check on transplanting. If you order by mail and receive a tree which is lacking any fibrous roots, demand your money back.

A selection of trees

To help you choose a shade-giving tree for your site, the following selection has been divided between trees that are remarkable for their foliage or bark, those that bear flowers or fruit, and trees that are most suitable for larger gardens.

Smaller trees for foliage or bark

Acer. Many maples have a graceful branch structure and elegant foliage casting a light shade. Most color brilliantly in the fall. The snakebarks remain attractive in winter with their striated bark; all make trees of modest size, but are not too slow-growing; they are hardy and easy to grow in any reasonable garden soil. Among the best are *A. capillipes*, with green, white-streaked bark, red young shoots and bright fall foliage; *A. davidii* and its cultivars, with green or red bark striped with white, and polished leaves that color vividly in the fall amid hanging bunches of red-

Planting a tree

If you have, or have created, the ideal soil for shade plants, you can set new small plants straight into it with no preparation, simply watering them in to ensure the mixture is in intimate contact with their roots. When planting trees or shrubs, however, you will need to take more trouble; the less welcoming your soil, the more effort it is worth putting in at the planting stage.

Dig a hole large enough to take the roots fully spread out; cramped roots may never take firm hold, and the tree's growth may be stunted. Loosen the subsoil, using a pick if need be to break through any hard pan of soil beneath the surface, and remove rocks or large stones.

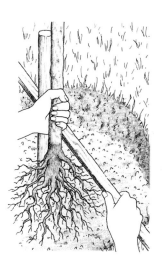

LEFT *The weeping silver pear,* Pyrus salicifolia *'Pendula,' once it has grown out of its spindly youth, makes a good canopy for shade-loving plants, provided you train it on a stem to allow light in beneath its trailing branches. Here, Lenten roses (*Helleborus orientalis*) in harmonious shades contribute to a gentle color scheme. It is worth cutting away the winter-damaged leaves of the hellebores before the flowering stems are too far advanced, so that the nodding blooms have the stage to themselves. If you leave the seedheads to form, you will soon have a colony of self-sown seedlings.*

Set the tree in the prepared hole, using a piece of wood to line up the old soil mark level with the surface. Spread the roots outwards. Set the stake—to which your tree will be tethered until the roots have taken hold—to windward of the tree and knock in the stake.

If the roots have been damaged, first cut ragged roots cleanly back past the wounded area. Then remove or shorten some of the tree's branches (see page 20) to restore the balance between root and top growth.

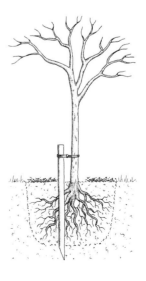

After cleaning up the roots and spreading them out, fill back with the soil mixture, teasing it among the roots. Firm it well with the heel of your boot, and water in thoroughly. Finally, spread a mulch, keeping it clear of the trunk; this will retain moisture and discourage weeds.

flushed, winged seeds; *A. pensylvanicum*, with a vibrant yellow fall color and handsome green stems which are striped with white; the taller *A. rufinerve*, with green and white bark bloomed with white on the young shoots, and fall foliage coloring to red and gold; and *A. tegmentosum*, whose green and purple stems have vertically running white fissures. *A. griseum*, the paperbark maple, has a shaggy trunk with peeling, mahogany bark, and leaves composed of three leaflets which take on rich scarlet tints in the fall. If you grow them in acid soil, all of these make good companions for rhododendrons, the solidity of the evergreen shrubs contrasting with the lightness and grace of the maples. On lime soils you could choose from the selection of evergreen shrubs on pages 44–5 to give a similar effect of a solid base and airy canopy. Keep the planting low around *A. griseum*, so that its beautiful shredding bark is not hidden.

The Japanese maple, *Acer japonicum aureum* (now correctly *A. shirasawanum aureum*), though very slow, is always beautiful, its fresh, lime-yellow foliage making the perfect contrast to a rhododendron with tan felting on the reverse of the leaves, such as *Rhododendron bureavii*. The golden maple itself needs some shade to save the leaves from sun-scorch. A Japanese species, *A. palmatum*, offers many spectacular selections whose beautiful foliage and outstanding colors are on display from spring to fall.

Azara microphylla. Somewhat frost-tender and rather slow-growing, this is a graceful tree for small gardens where the climate permits, with fan sprays of tiny evergreen leaves and minute yellow winter flowers smelling strongly of vanilla custard.

Betula. Although birches have greedy fibrous roots, they are such pretty trees, with their white or colored trunks and leaves pattering down like yellow coins in the fall, that it is hard to resist them. They grow fairly rapidly to medium-size, but their light canopy makes them suitable for smallish gardens nonetheless. *B. pendula* is the silver birch of circumpolar northern woodlands, and 'Laciniata' has deeply cut leaves. The North American paper birch, *B. papyrifera*, is whiter in bark. *B. nigra* 'Heritage,' a selection of the North American river birch, has lustrous, dark green leaves and shedding, buckskin-brown bark.

Asiatic birches include *B. albo-sinensis* with apricot-tan bark, and the very white *B. utilis jacquemontii*. Birches do well in most soils, whether they are moist or dry, but are not at their best in alkaline soils. Given sufficient moisture and acid soil, nothing is prettier than a birch (or even a grove of birches) underplanted with white, pink and crimson evergreen azaleas.

Elaeagnus angustifolia. The Russian olive is tough and indestructible in cold, heat, drought or wind. Lop the lower branches to make a small shade tree with gray-white leaves like an olive (though deciduous) borne on spiny stems, and sweetly fragrant, pale yellow flowers in early summer. Any soil except thin alkaline ones is suitable. Use it as shade for pale, pretty schemes, or contrast it with solid, dark evergreen foliage chosen from the selection of evergreen shrubs and ground-cover later in this chapter.

Gleditsia triacanthos. The honey locust is very spiny and grows large in time; try to obtain the thornless 'Inermis,' or one with colored leaves: 'Sunburst' in spring yellow, or 'Rubylace' in red, aging to bronzed green. The foliage is much more refined than that of the related black locust, *Robinia pseudoacacia*, and casts a dappled shade. Those with colored leaves are more restrained in growth, making them suitable for small gardens. For a symphony in chartreuse-yellow, pair *Gleditsia triacanthos* 'Sunburst' with *Catalpa bignonioides* 'Aurea.'

Metasequoia glyptostroboides. The dawn redwood, a deciduous conifer with fresh, soft green foliage turning to russet in the fall, is friendly to under-plantings in youth but less so as it matures: the carpet of fallen needles from a mature tree is thick and dense, stifling anything that grows beneath the branches. It appreciates moist soil, and grows quickly to form a medium-sized tree.

Olea europaea. The olive will often reach a great age, and grows tall where it receives ample moisture, but remains stunted in dry conditions. It will stand very little frost, but is one of the most characteristic trees of Mediterranean or Californian climes, with its grayish cast and the gnarled trunk it acquires with age. A typically Mediterranean-style underplanting would include blue and white *Anemone blanda* or the similar *A. apennina* and bunch-headed narcissi.

Roscoea cautleoides
A near-hardy relative of the edible ginger, it grows wild in the foothills of the Himalayas and is able to survive quite cold winters if given a thick mulch in the fall. It is happy in any cool, leafy soil that does not dry out. Its hooded, orchid-like, lemon-yellow flowers are borne in early summer on 1½ft stems over the narrow, upward-pointing leaves.

LEFT *The European whitebeams (*Sorbus aria *and cultivars) are alkaline-loving trees, beautiful in spring as their white-backed leaves unfurl buds as slender as candle flames; from a distance their poise recalls the white chalices of a magnolia. The flat heads of creamy flowers are followed by deep red fruits among the tawny gold fall leaves. But in springtime there is just the quiet harmony of gray and white, here spread over a carpet of English bluebells in a grassy turf. In the garden blue-flowered* Omphalodes cappadocica, *or grape hyacinths (*Muscari*), would be easier to control than the English bluebells.*

LEFT *A many-stemmed cherry spreads its branches over a fresh border planting of the frothy, lime-green flowers of lady's mantle* (Alchemilla mollis), *golden-leaved hostas, and* Geranium *'Johnson's Blue.'*

RIGHT *An old, hollow-stemmed fruit tree lends character as well as shade to this planting of Spanish bluebells,* Hosta sieboldiana *and the slender green spires of* Tellima grandiflora. *Climbing roses will add color in the tree canopy as summer advances.*

TREES TO AVOID AS SHADE-GIVERS

Horse chestnut, sycamore maple, beech, evergreen oak, poplar, plane, Norway maple and sugar maples, *Magnolia grandiflora*, paulownia, yew and many pines all have greedy roots, or a dense canopy excluding light and rain, or leaves that lie chokingly on the ground after falling; some have all three. If you have any of these trees, turn to the earlier chapter, "How much shade?" (see page 13), for ideas on how to cope with them.

Sorbus. This genus includes the whitebeams and the mountain ashes. The whitebeams, small to medium-sized trees, have undivided leaves, often white felted beneath, held like candle flames in spring. The European *S. aria* has extra-bold foliage in 'Majestica,' and young leaves as soft as cream plush in 'Lutescens.' *S. alnifolia* has a neat, rounded form and colored bark. The flowers of early summer are followed by orange-brown leaves and scarlet fruits in the fall. Good companions are other alkaline-soil plants such as box (*Buxus*) and phillyrea, whose dark, foliage contrasts with the pale whitebeam's.

Taxodium distichum. The bald cypress is a deciduous conifer similar to the dawn redwood (*Metasequoia glyptostroboides*) but much more refined in leaf. The foliage turns to russet and bronze in the fall. Though it grows well in ordinary garden soil, the bald cypress is well suited to wet soils, where it can be joined by candelabra and Sikkimensis primulas, *Iris sibirica* and other moisture-lovers.

Flowering or fruiting trees

Amelanchier. With starry white flowers in spring, and bright fall foliage, *A. canadensis* and its kin are ideal, quick-growing trees for small gardens. They are hardy and do well in most soils except strongly alkaline ones. They are charming underplanted with the sharp colors of spring—spurges such as *Euphorbia polychroma*, doronicums with cheery yellow daisies, the golden grass *Milium effusum aureum*, and small daffodils. In acid soils amelanchier is the ideal companion for pink azaleas.

Cercis. The Judas tree of Europe, *C. siliquastrum*, and the North American redbud, *C. canadensis*, bear their magenta-rose pea flowers in spring, on the bare branches and even the trunk, before the heart-shaped leaves unfurl. They are small trees which do best in well-drained soil, and their canopy casts a light shade. You could add more of their potent coloring with a Mediterranean-style underplanting of the bright magenta-pink *Anemone blanda* 'Radar.'

Cornus. Several of the dogwoods are enchanting small trees with showy white or pink bracts in late spring. They all tend to be shallow-rooting, so the soil rich in organic matter that is ideal for shade plants suits them very well. Except for *C. kousa*, they grow equally well in acid or alkaline soils. For continental climates *C. florida* from the eastern states of North America is the best; there are several cultivars in white or pink, charming as companions to white azaleas. The Japanese *C. kousa* and Chinese *C. kousa chinensis* (which is more lime-tolerant) need a moister, maritime climate. All color brightly in the fall. For mild areas there is the evergreen *C. capitata*, which has creamy primrose bracts and strawberry-like fruits similar to *C. kousa*'s. The hardy *C. controversa* displays the generic tendency to a tabular, tiering quality very markedly, and its flowers are an ivory-tinted froth.

Crataegus. The colored thorns, *C. laevigata* 'Paul's Scarlet' and 'Rosea Flore Pleno,' are popular small garden trees, though the old ladyish colors of the dull crimson and musty pink flowers they bear in spring are hard to place; above all, avoid them anywhere near yellow or orange. Their rather domesticated air harmonizes with old-fashioned plants such as columbines, bleeding heart and forget-me-nots. *C. phaenopyrum*, the Washington hawthorn, has white flowers and produces shiny, red fruits. Any reasonable garden soil suits the thorns.

Fraxinus. The manna ashes, medium-sized *F. ornus* and the smaller *F. mariesii* bear foamy, fragrant cream flowers in early summer. For the larger ashes, see "Trees for larger gardens" on pages 38–9.

Koelreuteria paniculata. The golden rain tree stands winter cold and welcomes a summer baking to encourage its bright yellow spires of flower in summer. Papery orange bladder-like seed capsules follow. The pinnate leaves resemble those of ash or mountain ash. It grows to medium size, forming a broad crown with time, and has no fads about soil.

Laburnum. To be avoided where children play, for they have poisonous seeds, the golden chains grow in cooler zones and bear their yellow tassels in late spring or early summer. *L. × watereri* 'Vossii' is the safest, as it bears the fewest seeds. With this proviso, the laburnums are ideal small garden trees.

RIGHT *This* Magnolia × soulangeana *has the clean, bold branches and white, wine-stained chalices typical of this most easygoing of the magnolias. A simple underplanting of deep blue polyanthus, their rich coloring enlivened by the yellow eye of each flower, is sufficiently discreet not to distract from the magnolia's uncluttered elegance and the play of light and shadow over its branches.*

Magnolia. The cultivars of *M. × soulangeana* are tougher than their looks suggest, with clean bold branches and white, pink or wine-purple chalice-shaped flowers in spring. Often grown as large shrubs, they can be limbed up with care to make a multi-stemmed tree suitable for underplanting. *M. salicifolia* is a slender small tree with small, pure white flowers smelling of orange blossom and opening in spring on the bare branches, followed by neat leaves which cast a dappled shade. The Loebneri hybrids are similar, and cope with alkaline conditions so long as the soil is moist: 'Leonard Messel' has ivory flowers suffused with pink, 'Merrill' has starry white blooms. Any of the spring-flowering magnolias is enchanting with an underplanting of blue *Omphalodes cappadocica* or grape hyacinths. The summer magnolias, such as *M. sieboldii* (for acid soils) and the lime-tolerant *M. wilsonii*, grow fast in ideal conditions and bear their fragrant, nodding, white, crimson-hearted blooms from an early age.

Malus. The crab apples are attractive small flowering trees, adaptable to a wide range of soils and climates, which also flower late enough to escape spring frosts in treacherous climates. *M.* 'Profusion' has foliage which is a reddish-purple in color and deep red flowers. This crab apple also produces dark wine-red fruits. *M. floribunda*, immensely popular for its chintzy red buds opening to pink and fading to white, weeps almost to the ground. Fruiting crabs such as *M.* 'John Downie,' bearing fruits which make delicious jelly, can be as pretty as any ornamental crab when in flower. They grow in a similar way to an orchard apple, and like orchard apple trees they make charming companions for primroses and violets.

Oxydendrum arboreum. The sourwood or sorrel tree is a small tree for acid soils only. With its slender outline, sprays of white bells in summer and brilliant scarlet fall color, it is an ideal companion for rhododendrons or azaleas.

Prunus. Here belong the ubiquitous Japanese cherries, which range from an overbearing flounce of sugar pink to the dignity of *P.* 'Tai Haku,' the great white cherry, with its single white flowers and bronzed young growth. *P.* 'Ukon' is also admissible for the sake of its flowers of palest primrose-green. If you choose a pink cherry, its coloring will be set off best by the cool tones of gray rock, blue-gray conifers or the distant purple haze of birchwoods; red brick and the acid greens of spring do not flatter its sugar-pink blossom. Pale pink cherries are easier to place. The Japanese cherries mostly make small trees, varying in habit from low and spreading to narrowly upright or vase-shaped.

Certain wild cherries and their near descendants have greater charm. *Prunus sargentii*, with single pink flowers and coppery young growth, forms a small, round-headed tree with the additional attraction of bright fall tints; an underplanting of *Geranium macrorrhizum* 'Album,' with white flowers in pink calyces, works well with it. *P. serrula*, with undistinguished flowers and narrow leaves, is appreciated for its bark, as polished as mahogany; keep the underplanting low and simple not to detract from its beauty. The hybrids 'Accolade' in bright pink, 'Kursar' in deep pink or 'Okame' in carmine are all excellent small trees which flower in early spring. A grouping of *Rhododendron* 'Praecox,' very early-flowering with dainty, purple flowers, purple *Daphne mezereum*, a pink *Pieris japonica*, and *Bergenia purpurascens* will create an extraordinary color interaction with *Prunus* 'Okame,' the varying purple and pink shades of the underplanting seeming to shift the color of the blossom towards a clean pink. The winter cherry, *P. subhirtella* 'Autumnalis,' is valued for its unusual flowering season; in spring it would turn no heads, and the pink form is hardly showier, but in midwinter the delicate blossom on bare branches is charming. The winter cherries are graceful small trees giving pleasant shade, and less greedy at the roots than the Japanese cherries. An underplanting of variegated hostas, ferns and epimediums would give year-round interest.

Schinus molle. The pepper tree is for mild climates, as it will stand only a touch of frost. Its narrowly laddering fronds of evergreen foliage cast a pleasant shade, but the roots grow massive with age though the tree itself remains of modest size. Strings of bright pink fruits like peppercorns borne by the female trees account for the popular name. It is common in Mediterranean areas and California as a street tree.

TREES THAT WILL STAND SHADE

If your garden is already shaded, it can be helpful to know which trees you can expect to do well.

● Laburnum seems to flower as abundantly under a canopy of taller trees (such as London plane) as in the open.

● *Styrax japonicus* and *Oxydendron arboreum* prefer light shade and woodland soil, and so do the stewartias, camellia relatives with small white flowers and flaking, marbled bark.

● Japanese maples color best in full sun but appreciate wind shelter and dappled shading, as do flowering dogwoods.

● The deciduous *Eucryphia glutinosa*, a small, open-branched tree with white flowers in summer filled with a puff of stamens, prefers a leafy, neutral to acid soil and light shade.

● Magnolias—except for *M. × soulangeana*, which seems to stand anything so long as the soil is neutral to acid—are at their happiest in part shade with their roots in cool soil rich in organic matter. They prefer never to be disturbed once planted.

Sorbus. Some mountains ashes have orange or red fruits, and are generally a promiscuous bunch producing who knows what from seed while others have white or pink fruits and keep themselves to themselves so that seedlings resemble the parent tree. They are all small to medium-sized trees. The orange fruits of the common mountain ash, *S. aucuparia*, ripen in summer and are quickly stripped by the birds. *S. aucuparia* 'Beissneri' has bright winter bark of coral and red, and *S. aucuparia* 'Aspleniifolia' has deeply cut, lacy leaves. Oriental mountain ashes with scarlet or orange fruits include *S. commixta*, which is very bright in leaf and fruit, and *S. discolor*, with large white flowers and bright scarlet fruits. *Stewartia.* These long-lived, ornamental shrubs and small trees make excellent specimen plants for the shady garden. As well as brightly colored foliage in the fall, many stewartias develop handsome bark with maturity. They prefer moist, well-drained, acidic soil which is rich in organic matter and do best in an open or partly shaded site. The Japanese stewartia, *S. pseudocamellia*, a medium-sized tree with peeling bark, has white flowers with orange anthers and turns to fiery shades in the fall. *S. koreana*, the Korean stewartia, has flaking, orange-brown bark and white flowers with yellow stamens. The foliage turns red-purple in the fall. *S. monodelpha*, another Japanese species, is rounded in shape. It has richly colored brown bark which becomes smooth with age. The white, cup-shaped flowers are long-lasting and in the fall the foliage is a striking, maroon-red in color.

Styrax japonicus. A graceful and friendly shade-maker with open, fan-like branches and small leaves, the snowbell tree bears its white bells in summer. It appreciates ideal shade-garden soil, rich in organic matter and without lime. Rhododendrons with bold foliage make ideal companions for the elegant growth of the snowbell tree.

Trees for larger gardens

Ailanthus altissima. The tree of heaven is big and very fast-growing, quite unsuitable for a small garden but valuable because it will grow in almost any climate and almost any soil, and is tolerant of air pollution. The ash-like foliage is formed of many bold leaflets; some female trees are handsome when bearing their clusters of bright rust-red fruits.

Fraxinus. Ash trees are mostly big and quite fast-growing, with ample, pinnate foliage casting deepish shade in summer, and as they are late in coming into leaf, early spring woodlanders have time to flower and mature before they block out the light. The common ash, *F. excelsior*, is far too big for most gardens. *F. angustifolia* is only slightly smaller, and makes a fast-growing and elegant tree for a large garden; *F. angustifolia* 'Raywood' owes its common name, the claret ash, to its rich fall color.

RIGHT *Laburnum is aptly nicknamed golden chain on account of its graceful tassles of yellow pea-flowers. Laburnum is not only a shade-giver, but shade-tolerant too, flowering as freely beneath a canopy of taller trees as in the open garden. It lends itself to training onto a metal or wooden framework, and can be used to create a laburnum tunnel, a shadowy green walkway magical with golden blossom in spring. The bold fern fronds make a fresh green underplanting.*

Pruning for shapely growth

Newly planted trees, or saplings inherited with a new garden, always repay thoughtful pruning. Trained well from the start, they should grow into graceful mature trees which cast the kind of dappled shade valued by every shade-gardener. Keep pruning every year or two, in the spring, as the tree develops to maintain an open, branching structure and a clean, uncluttered trunk.

Remove any branchlets springing so low that if they were left the tree would look more like a shrub.

Eliminate crossing branches; take out the one growing inwards first, and decide later if you need to remove the other as well, now or in the future.

Quercus. The oaks include some of the finest shade-giving trees, for their deep roots are no threat to underplantings. *Q. robur* and *Q. petraea* are the English and durmast oaks of the Old World, full of character as they age, but forest rather than garden trees. *Q. rubra*, the red oak, *Q. palustris*, the pin oak, and especially *Q. coccinea*, the scarlet oak, are splendid fall-coloring trees with boldly lobed leaves. They all grow quickly in good soil and become large in maturity, so they are unsuitable for small gardens. Where space allows, however, they are the best of canopies for choice rhododendrons.

Robinia pseudoacacia. The black locust is a sizable, fast-growing tree with a highly decorative pattern of foliage, but it has a tendency to produce suckers which makes it less than ideal for shade gardening. The white, faintly scented flowers are borne in long sprays at midsummer. *R. pseudoacacia* 'Frisia' is the popular golden version, but the yellow-leaved honey locust, *Gleditsia triacanthos*, is a far prettier tree. An underplanting of spurges, pale daffodils and variegated comfrey echoes the fresh tones of *Robinia pseudoacacia* 'Frisia.'

Sophora japonica. The Japanese pagoda tree is attractive in leaf, and even more so when bearing its ivory pea flowers in summer. These need the encouragement of long hot summers and are not borne on young trees. It grows quite large in time, making a suitable canopy for bold-leaved evergreen shrubs.

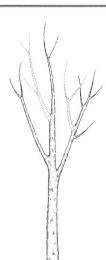

Decide which branch is the leader, and give it a clear start by removing any branches that might compete with it, especially those that threaten to form a trunk with a narrow V—always a weak point.

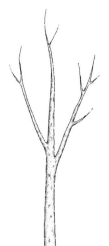

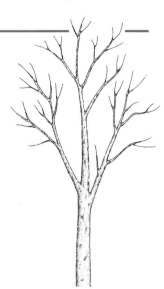

Unless you have invested in a standard or semi-standard tree, the lowest branches that you will leave at this stage may be no more than 3–4ft from the ground. As the tree grows, take off these branches to leave a clear trunk of 6–8ft, maybe more if the tree will naturally grow very tall in time.

Planting an exotic woodland

"Woodland," in this context, does not mean acres: it could be suggested by just one or two trees, so long as the soil beneath and the canopy above create conditions similar to a woodland margin. An exotic woodland planting acknowledges the artificiality of the micro-environment, but you need to work within its limitations.

Consider, also, the visual setting. Does your tree suggest a color scheme in the blue half of the spectrum, or the yellow? Pink cherries call for blues, mauves, glaucous foliage; trees with acid-yellow spring foliage blend with scarlet, fresh green and yellow. Trees with white flowers or neutral green foliage give you greater freedom of choice.

ABOVE **Left to right:**
Rhododendron **Fabia,**
Dryopteris affinis, Pieris
'Firecrest,'
Gymnocarpium
dryopteris, Gaultheria
procumbens **(around tree**
trunk).

For acid soil,
beneath a scarlet oak

Choose from the plants listed below and let the shrubs and ferns rise from a leafy floor; rhododendrons especially prefer not to have their rootball covered. This group is based on clear scarlet and fresh greens; for a softer note you could add the dainty *Corylopsis pauciflora* with primrose bells and coral spring foliage, or *Fothergilla gardenii*, which has cream, fuzzy bottlebrush flowers and bright fall tints.

Gaultheria procumbens: creeping growth forming ground-cover of glossy dark green leaves; small white flowers followed by bright scarlet berries in the fall.
Pieris 'Firecrest': young growth in spring coral-scarlet, fading through apricot and lemon to green; sprays of urn-shaped white flowers in spring.
Rhododendron Fabia: a wide mound; coral-orange bells mid-season.
Dryopteris affinis: bold deep green fronds unfurling from golden croziers in spring.
Gymnocarpium dryopteris (oak fern): fresh green, very lacy deciduous fronds.

ABOVE left to right:
Ribes laurifolium,
Helleborus orientalis (at
back), *Primula vulgaris*
and *Galanthus nivalis*
(at front), *Polypodium*
vulgare 'Cornubiense'
(by tree trunk and
half-right).

For limy soil,
beneath a white cherry

Within this framework you can build on the
theme of white and green as far as space
permits, with snowdrops and white Lenten
roses, polypody ferns, white and cream
primroses and Solomon's seal, white dicentras
and white-variegated hostas, white martagon
lilies, and in the fall white willow gentian
and *Actaea alba* or white baneberry, with its
red-stalked white fruits.

Ribes laurifolium: low and spreading, with
large, toothed leaves; nodding sprays of ivory-
green flowers very early in the year.
Polypodium vulgare 'Cornubiense': divided
fronds, spring fresh in summer.
Helleborus orientalis: nodding saucer flowers
ranging from white through pink to plum.
Galanthus nivalis: the common snowdrop,
with single or double, white, green-marked
flowers.
Primula vulgaris: the common primrose, with
pale yellow, or occasionally cream, flowers.

Enduring foliage and form

Within the shelter of shade-giving trees, the garden needs a firm structure of shrubs, ferns and ground-cover to frame the more ephemeral incidents of flower and berry. Where the climate permits, ever-green shrubs provide an especially valuable contrast in winter with the tracery of leafless trees, saving the garden from looking derelict during the cold months and helping in turn to provide further shelter for the small treasures described in later chapters.

Unless otherwise noted, the shrubs described on the following pages will grow perfectly satisfactorily without regular pruning. It may sometimes be necessary to control their growth, which is best done by tracing individual branches back to their point of origin and cutting them out completely. Avoid at all costs the "clipped ball" style of pruning, which scarcely merits the word, as it consists of uniform cutting back without regard for the nature of each shrub. It deprives the plant of its character and may rob you of the pleasure of its flowers as well.

Even shrubs that grow reasonably fast can look very small in the early stages, and it is tempting to plant them closely to achieve your framework effects quickly. Although convention urges you not to succumb to this temptation, with rare exceptions I believe it is perfectly acceptable, provided–and it is an important proviso–you keep watch for overcrowd-ing, and are prepared to move some of the shrubs to new positions as they grow, or even to scrap the least attractive and let the best take over. To cut down on expense and waste, you could begin a new garden by planting just one smallish area and leaving the rest down to grass, creating a new bed only when you need to move some shrubs; in this way the new area you are planting will look surprisingly mature from the very start.

Most shrubs can be moved satisfactorily as long as they are not too big for you to handle without strain, and you prepare the new site for them in advance of moving them, and lift them carefully without damaging the roots, retaining the root ball and its soil intact as far as possible. It is often worth watering shrubs before lifting, and in any case be sure to water them very thoroughly after moving. Moving shrubs is ideally done at the same season as planting (see page 30). In their first season after transplanting, shrubs are likely to appreciate extra wind shelter and daily syringing with water in hot or dry spells, which will help to reduce moisture loss through the leaves and stems.

Among the most suitable shrubs for this treat-ment are the evergreen azaleas and small rhodo-dendrons; these are practically portable, so readily do they settle in after a move if treated properly. Buy as many as you can afford, plant them closely to form a thicket, and move every alternate one to a new home as they begin to grow into each other. Shrubs that are unsuitable for moving once planted are those with taproots, such as brooms, or with fleshy roots that are easily damaged, such as magnolias.

BELOW *Two colorful forms of ivy*–Hedera helix *'Buttercup' in its adult, golden form and* H. helix *'Marginata Major' boldly edged with white–swarm up the dark Chinese juniper (*Juniperus chinensis*) in a garden picture that will last in beauty all year.*

In this spring grouping the Skimmia japonica *on the left is in flower, but all year it will make a neat dome of evergreen foliage contrasting with the gold and green* Euonymus fortunei *in front. On the right, the bright drumstick flowers of* Primula denticulata.

Evergreen shrubs

Easy evergreens such as spotted laurel (*Aucuba japonica*) and the cherry and Portugal laurels (*Prunus laurocerasus* and *P. lusitanica*), the dumpy *Viburnum davidii*, and even privet (*Ligustrum ovalifolium*) have their value in the shade garden. Some forms of the spotted laurel–especially those without spots–are handsome, medium-sized shrubs: *Aucuba japonica* 'Salicifolia' is a female form with slender, polished leaves and abundant red fruits, matched in leaf by the male *A. japonica* 'Lance Leaf,' while *A. japonica* 'Crassifolia' is a male with thick-textured, broad, deep green leaves. Although they will cope with almost any conditions of cold, wind and rooty soil, they will reward you generously if you treat them well. They are ideal for making a base of solid greenery beneath open-canopied trees, or for forming bays and promontories; smaller or more ephemeral shade-lovers from the chapters on the decor and cameos and collectibles (see pages 59 and 83) could be planted in the bays.

The ordinary cherry laurel is a very big shrub with glossy bold leaves, handsome and useful as a windbreak beneath tall trees. The finest foliage belongs to *Prunus laurocerasus* 'Magnoliifolia.' The low, spreading cultivars belong later in this chapter among shrubs for ground-cover (see page 53). All cherry laurels bear creamy flower spikes with a not quite nice smell in spring.

Another evergreen shrub with light-reflecting leaves is *Phillyrea latifolia*, a good companion for whitebeams; a large shrub, it is elegant in leaf if not very exciting in its white flowers. This is one shrub which lends itself well to the Victorian treatment of clipping to shape, allowing it to be grown in smallish spaces. The related osmanthuses, medium-sized shrubs more suited to smaller gardens even when left unpruned, range from the worthy *Osmanthus burkwoodii* to the holly-leaved *O. heterophyllus*. One of the best for shade is *O. decorus*, a broad dome of a shrub with bold, shiny leaves and small white fragrant flowers in spring.

Skimmias are a touch more persnickety than these undemanding evergreens. They need a moist, leafy soil, neutral or acid for preference, and shade; in sun

or dry soil they can easily turn a chlorotic yellow. Like spotted laurel, they come in male and female forms: the males are superior in flower and fragrance, the females are showy when wearing their bright scarlet baubles. Most are small shrubs, and some are very compact or even dwarf in size. *Skimmia japonica* 'Rubella' is a male cultivar with deep crimson-red winter buds opening to ivory flowers in spring, which looks charming with white narcissi; *S. japonica* 'Fragrans' is less showy in winter but superior in lily-of-the-valley perfume as the flowers open. For smaller spaces 'Ruby Dome' resembles a half-sized 'Rubella.' 'Nymans' is an excellent, free-fruiting female. The wide-spreading growth of *S. × confusa* 'Kew Green' is set with cones of alabaster-white flowers amid bright green leaves. It can form the centerpiece of a green and white scheme for late winter and spring, with snowdrops or *Leucojum vernum* and green hellebores, followed by white-variegated hostas for summer.

ABOVE *Daphniphyllum macropodum* is a noble evergreen foliage shrub with some of the poise of a rhododendron, but tolerant of lime soils. The red leaf stalks add a touch of color all year, and in the fall blue, bloomy fruits follow the insignificant flowers.

RIGHT *One of the finest white camellias for the shady garden is 'Cornish Snow,' a hardy, shapely shrub with pink-tinted buds opening to pure white flowers over a long season, and copper-tinted young foliage in spring.*

The yellow bells of *Mahonia japonica*, borne in sprays in winter, are also graced with a lily-of-the-valley perfume. This forms a medium-sized, mounded shrub, and can be kept well-clothed with foliage if you are ruthless about cutting back leggy stems from time to time. The hybrids of this and *M. lomariifolia* (a tall, gangly shrub for milder places, with ruffs of hard-textured leaflets) are more showy in flower, but I know of only one with a noticeable fragrance, *M. × media* 'Winter Sun.' The popular *M.* 'Charity' has little. All have leaves composed of several holly-like leaflets. The smaller mahonias have a different appeal; *M. nervosa* slowly creeps to make ground-cover, its spine-toothed leaflets making a distinctive pattern. It deserves the simplest of accompanying planting: moss, the arching plumes of *Danae racemosa* and fall cyclamen are all excellent partners for this mahonia.

In place of the more common *Viburnum davidii* I would choose *V. cinnamomifolium*, a taller and more open shrub with similarly bold and deeply grooved leaves, more highly polished than those of *V. davidii*. Other less familiar but very decorative evergreens for shady places are *Trochodendron aralioides*, which has pale green leaves thinly margined with russet, held in whorls on long stalks; and the Florida anise, *Illicium floridanum*, an aromatic, fast-growing shrub with gleaming, thick-textured, bright green leaves and red, starry flowers in spring. Both form medium-sized shrubs.

Another unusual and highly decorative evergreen shrub for soil rich in organic matter in dappled or part-shade is *Daphniphyllum macropodum*. The leaves, which are glaucous-backed, are borne on markedly pink petioles, the color extending up the midrib and giving it something of the air of a rhododendron such as *Rhododendron fortunei*. The daphniphyllum has insignificant flowers, but earns its keep twelve months of the year with such foliage.

The lusterleaf holly, *Ilex latifolia*, with lustrous, dark green leaves, is a very shade-tolerant shrub, handsome in itself and as a backdrop for pale flowers. For a sheltered place in light shade, *Itea ilicifolia* is a shrub of distinction with holly-like foliage—though lacking the fierce spines—and attractive green-cream catkin-like tassles of fragrant flowers in summer.

45

A green and shady courtyard

In many areas influenced by Muslim culture a secluded courtyard with plants, and often a fountain or bubbling pool, is an integral part of the dwelling house. In hot countries the courtyard is designed to offer welcome shade from the sun as well as privacy. Even in cities many a town house has a basement "area" which with imagination can be transformed into the semblance of a courtyard. Here, though, the challenge will be to bring more light into a dark place. Whitewashed walls or mirrors can help to give an illusion of greater space and reflect more light into the darkest corners.

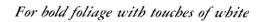

For bold foliage with touches of white

Fatsia japonica: bold palmate leaves of dark shining green with undulate margins; umbels of ivory flowers in the fall. Suitable for any reasonable soil, grows well in containers and can be hard-pruned if it gets too large—it can grow to 8ft. Remove lower branches to make room for shade plants at its feet.
Galanthus 'S. Arnott': one of the noblest of the snowdrops.
Hosta undulata undulata: smallish, rather narrow, twisted leaves, green with broad white central markings.
Polystichum setiferum: a member of the Plumoso-Divisilobum group which has swirling, divided, ruffled foliage.

ABOVE **From left to right:** *Polystichum setiferum* **Plumoso-Divisilobum,** *Hosta undulata undulata,* **another polystichum,** *Fatsia japonica.*
RIGHT **On the wall, left to right:** *Itea ilicifolia, Berberidopsis corallina*; **in front,** *Polystichum falcatum* 'Rochfordiana,' *Dicentra macrantha, Adiantum venustum, Viola hederacea* **with** *Daphne odora* **behind.**

For a green and white composition in a smaller space

Bergenia stracheyi var. *alba*: small, leathery, rounded leaves; short stems topped with heads of white or faintly blush flowers in spring.

Choisya ternata: aromatic, shining dark green trifoliate leaves; heads of fragrant white flowers in spring, often with a fall repeat, on a rounded shrub 6ft high and wide.

Iris foetidissima 'Variegata': evergreen sword leaves, green striped with white.

Viola obliqua alba: a scentless violet with wide, butterfly-like blooms of pure white.

RIGHT *Choisya ternata* underplanted with, left and right, *Viola obliqua alba* and *Iris foetidissima* 'Variegata,' and *Bergenia stracheyi* var. *alba* in the center.

For a sheltered corner

Adiantum venustum: dainty maidenhair fern, which slowly increases at the root.

Daphne odora 'Alba': low, wide bush of polished, blunt-ended green leaves; creamy-white flowers in spring, deliciously fragrant.

Dicentra macrantha: beautiful, non-climbing perennial with divided leaves of pale, fresh green, and amber yellow lockets growing on 1½ ft stems in spring; needs space in cool shade.

Itea ilicifolia: holly-like leaves, long tassles of catkin-like, green-white flowers in summer.

Polystichum falcatum 'Rochfordiana': finest of the holly ferns, with broad glossy pinnae.

Viola hederacea (chinless violet): lilac-blue and white flowers; spreads freely.

Evergreens for acid soils

BELOW Pieris japonica *is not one of the brightest Pieris in spring leaf, but its flowers are very fine, drooping sprays of white bells. Here they reach down to the bright purple, spurred flowers of a corydalis.*

Gardens with acid soils are easily dominated by one genus, *Rhododendron*. A selection is described in the chapter on key plants (see page 107). The easiest to grow—as undemanding as laurel, except for their insistence on lime-free soil—are the hardy hybrids, usually large shrubs with undistinguished foliage and showy trusses of flowers. The colors fall mainly in the range of white, pink, magenta and mauve; there are no pure reds (*R.* 'Scarlet Romance' is the nearest to a true scarlet) or true blues. Being so easy to grow, the hardy hybrids are useful as the first stage of planting in a garden not yet sheltered enough for better things, or as boundary plantings within which rhododendrons and other acid-loving shrubs of greater distinction can find protection.

Many rhododendron species are shrubs or trees of great beauty, but not all are easy to grow. When planting, take special care to set the rootball in leafy, acid soil with the surface of the rootball level with or partly above the soil surface, and after watering mulch with leaf mold or ground bark, so that moisture is retained but air can still reach the roots through the fluffy mulch. As well as their showy flowers, rhododendrons may also have striking bark or beautiful leaves, either exceptionally large or backed with silvery, fox-red or deep brown felt (indumentum), or sometimes both. The big-leaved rhododendrons need optimum conditions, cool and moist with high atmospheric humidity. Smaller-leaved species with striking indumentum on the reverse of the leaves are generally easier to grow.

The ideal compromise for most gardeners is the group of rhododendrons known as primary hybrids—meaning that both parents were a species—or those with at least one parent a species. They retain much of the elegance of the wild rhododendron, while often being better adapted to garden conditions. The famous Loderi rhododendrons are primary hybrids, while the scarlet-flowered *R. griersonianum* and yellow *R. campylocarpum* have passed their color to several offspring, such as coral-scarlet Fabia and the yellow 'Letty Edwards.'

Most other evergreen shrubs in the great family Ericaceae also require acid soil: *Kalmia latifolia* (which needs ample light to flower well in high latitudes), leucothoë, gaultheria and vaccinium. *Pieris* is a genus with an ever-increasing number of cultivars; some are grown mainly for their bright spring foliage, such as *Pieris formosa* var. *forrestii* 'Wakehurst' and the elegant 'Jermyns,' 'Firecrest,' 'Forest Flame' and 'Bert Chandler.' They grow large in time, so in small gardens the cultivars of *P. japonica*, a medium-sized shrub, may be more suitable. They are also generally more resistant to frost than the bigger pierises.

BELOW *Rhododendrons bring vivid color and solid evergreenery to the entrance of this porticoed house, and will thrive beneath the kindly dappled shade of a tree which will also help to cool the house in summer.*

With the odd exception such as 'Scarlett O'Hara,' *Pieris japonica* cultivars are not so bright in spring but have finer flowers. Good white-flowered cultivars include 'Purity' with rather upright sprays, and the elegant 'White Cascade'; 'Dorothy Wyckoff' and the very graceful 'Grayswood' have warm tan winter buds. Pink-flowered pierises are now readily available: 'Blush' and 'Pink Delight' are both mid-pink, 'Daisen' and 'Christmas Cheer' have maroon buds opening to pink flowers, and 'Flamingo' is deepest of all, with flowers the color of watered claret.

Camellias, too, need neutral to acid soil, and mostly thrive in light shade. They can grow large in time, but respond surprisingly well to cutting back to keep them compact enough for small spaces. Among the flowers of *Camellia japonica* cultivars you can find everything from single blooms simple as dog roses to doubles as formal as if carved from fine wax; most have glossy, broad leaves. *C. saluenensis*, which bears its pink funnels in late winter and early spring, is a plant of great quality, and the adorable *C. cuspidata*, though its ivory flowers are small, has the

added value of deep coppery-black spring growth. The two have been crossed to give 'Cornish Snow,' probably the best white camellia for the garden. *C. × williamsii*, the group of hybrids between *C. japonica* and *C. saluenensis*, also offer something for all tastes, as described in the chapter on key plants (see page 107). Those with single flowers, like *C. saluenensis*, make ideal woodland shrubs, even if your "woodland" is suggested by no more than one or two trees of undomesticated looks. The doubles look best in more formal settings. *C. sasanqua* and its hybrids are particularly hardy and early-flowering camellias.

The protea family is essentially for warm gardens only. If you can combine near frost-free conditions with shade and moisture, however, the Chilean hazel, *Gevuina avellana*, should grow for you. A tall shrub or tree with flexuous stems, it has foliage like a super-luxuriant mahonia but unarmed: deep green,

glossy and doubly or triply pinnate, with leaflets varying in size from a thumbnail to the palm of a hand. The flowers are thin spidery spikes of ivory, followed by fruits the size and color of red cherries and containing an edible nut.

Two shrubs with colored foliage enjoy similar conditions: *Cleyera fortunei* has smooth, pointed leaves marbled with gray and broadly margined with cream flushed pink, while *Pseudowintera colorata*, a New Zealander, has oval leaves of metallic old-gold above and steel blue beneath, flecked and stained with purple. I have seen it grow to 15ft tall, but it is very slow-growing except in its preferred conditions of moist, open-skied shade. These two choice shrubs and the Chilean hazel would make a trio of rare distinction for a warm, shaded garden with lime-free soil. Companion plants could include lapis-berried dianellas and frost-tender ferns.

ABOVE *Gevuina avellana, the Chilean hazel, is one of the noblest foliage plants for sheltered, shady places with high atmospheric humidity. This young plant, in the lee of a wall, will ultimately grow into a large shrub or even a tree. The grandest fronds of foliage are borne by plants growing strongly; as they mature to reach flowering age the leaves may become smaller.*

Deciduous shrubs of distinction

Though fine evergreens are the most important component of gardens in shade, at least where the winters are not too severe, some deciduous shrubs which offer more than just flower or fruit have sufficient presence to contribute to the framework, and not merely the decor, of the garden.

The most familiar hydrangeas, those with mopheads or lacecaps which vary from blue to pink as the soil pH increases, are pure decor. But *Hydrangea sargentiana*, which thrives even in dense shade so long as there is moisture, is a big shrub of considerable character. Its great leaves have the texture of deep green velvet, its stout stems are clad in bristly fur, and its flowers are hummocky aggregates of tiny purple florets surrounded by sparse white sterile florets sticking out like little feet. It does not lend itself to being crammed in among other plants: you need sufficient space to allow it to stand alone, underplanted with mosses and ferns.

Hydrangea aspera villosa, another big shrub, has less imposing foliage, but its lacecap flowers are more striking, with mauve-pink fertile florets surrounded by lilac-mauve sterile ones. Its color is unchanging whatever the soil.

For acid soils, few shrubs have more grace than *Clethra delavayi*, a tall, almost tree-like shrub with velvet-backed leaves and sprays of milk-white flowers held in silvered calyces that age to pink. An underplanting of *Helleborus lividus* would provide an evergreen echo of its grayish tones, with the bonus of dove-pink flowers in early spring; *Vaccinium glauco-album* (see page 123) is also in the same tender color range and needs the same leafy, acid soil as the clethra. Two handsome viburnums, also for lime-free soils only, are V. *furcatum* and V. *lantanoides* (syn. V. *alnifolium*). Both have bold, rounded leaves coloring richly in the fall to shades of claret and purple, and both grow slowly to medium size, though the first is more upright in growth.

Disanthus cercidifolius, a witch hazel relative which takes on similar deep tones in the fall, also has sizable, rounded leaves. Unlike most shrubs, it

seems to relish being crammed in among other plants. The witch hazels (*Hamamelis*) themselves make imposing shrubs in time: bold in leaf, they color to yellow, orange or red in the fall in rough correlation to their flower color, and in winter they bear their spidery, sharp-scented flowers. These are a delight to pick, but it is wise to restrain yourself to small twigs for posies as they are slow-growing and do not readily break into new growth where cut back. The original introduction of the Chinese witch hazel, *Hamamelis mollis*, named 'Coombe Wood' —still one of the finest, though it is seldom offered for sale—has large yellow flowers with a strong, sweet fragrance. Deeper tones belong to 'Gold-crest,' which flowers later, the rich yellow petals suffused with wine-red at the base, and to the chunky-flowered 'Brevipetala,' which approaches a warm orange in color.

ABOVE *One of the most distinguished of deciduous shrubs is* Hydrangea aspera sargentiana, *with its large, velvety, dark green leaves and flowerheads like little purple turtles. Here it grows behind* H. arborescens *'Annabelle,' left unpruned to produce small but abundant white flowerheads.*

Japan has its witch hazel too, *H. japonica*; smaller in leaf than the Chinese species, it has less fragrant flowers, the petals twisted and crumpled. Var. *arborea* is more tree-like than most witch hazels, and has a characteristic horizontal branching structure. The latest to flower of this group is 'Zuccariniana,' which has pale, sharp yellow flowers in early spring.

The hybrids between the Chinese and the Japanese witch hazels, known as *H. × intermedia*, offer several orange- or red-flowered cultivars, usually with cinnabar and coppery orange fall foliage to match. 'Jelena' has large coppery flowers, and 'Ruby Glow' is richer still, though nearer to tawny port than ruby. The deepest red, of the shade usually called oxblood, is 'Diane,' but 'Feuerzauber' ('Magic Fire'), though paler, is the only scented red. A carpet of crimson-leaved *Tellima grandiflora* 'Purpurea' at their feet would contribute to a winter scheme of unseasonal richness. One of the most beautiful of the hybrids is 'Pallida,' deliciously scented and far more alluring

than its name suggests, the flowers not pallid but a subtle shade of pale, clear lemon, best seen against a dark background, such as a hedge of yew (*Taxus baccata*). The newer 'Moonlight' is soft lemon, 'Primavera' is citron-yellow with crimson at the heart, and 'Sunburst' has long, scarcely twisted petals of vivid buttercup. The brightest in fall leaf is *H. vernalis* 'Sandra,' which has yellow flowers in winter, and young leaves expanding in shades of claret in spring.

In dappled or light shade, with plenty of organic matter in the soil, the witch hazels should do well in most soils except those with the highest pH levels. The same quality of soil suits *Hydrangea quercifolia*, a large shrub valued for its white lacecap flowers and for the rich fall tones of its bold, jagged-lobed leaves. Shrubs such as these blur the distinction between the framework and the decor of the garden, and some at least of the shrubs described in the next chapter on the decor (see page 59) could as well belong here.

BELOW *The yellow flowers of witch hazels* (Hamamelis) *appear on the bare branches in winter, and are at their best with a dark background to set them off. Slow-growing at first, witch hazels mature to form spreading shrubs and should be allowed to develop their natural outline, as they do not respond well to cutting back.*

RIGHT ABOVE *Ground-cover plants amid shrubs make a satisfying year-round picture. The large, leathery foliage of bergenias contrasts in scale with the rounded leaves of* Saxifraga umbrosa, *and in outline with the spear leaves of* Iris foetidissima *'Variegata.' Behind are silver-flecked* Brunnera macrophylla *'Langtrees,'* Helleborus argutifolius *and acanthus.*

RIGHT BELOW *The pale new leaves of* Epimedium perralderianum *unfurl against a backdrop of its own mature, dark foliage that here makes a solid base of weed-excluding foliage for the steeples of blue* Campanula latiloba *beneath an apple tree.*

Ground-cover

It may seem odd to include ground-cover in a chapter on the framework of the garden; however, ground-cover plants offer much more than just a way of excluding weeds. Rightly chosen, they play an important role in the design of the garden, unifying and linking groups of plants, and performing much the same role in the horizontal plane as evergreen shrubs perform in the vertical one (including, if appropriate to the design, clipped hedges).

In this aesthetic role, as opposed to the purely functional, the chief players will be low evergreen shrubs, for few non-woody perennials (even if evergreen) have sufficient presence to qualify. A significant exception are the bergenias, of which a selection is described in the chapter on key plants (see page 110). Their bold, leathery leaves give firmness and solidity to many a planting that might otherwise seem flimsy. They grow in almost any soil, take on

brightest winter leaf tones when touched by the sun for at least part of the day, and look especially well in formal or informal settings with stone.

The evergreen species of epimedium, equally efficient as weed excluders, give a different visual effect, forming patterns enhanced by the play of light reflecting on their polished leaflets. The almost circular or kidney-shaped leaves of *Asarum europaeum* also have a shiny surface, and this is a competent spreader in cool soils. The leathery, glossy leaves of *Galax urceolata* (syn. *G. aphylla*) are similarly rounded and take on tones of burnished mahogany in winter. Slim spikes of white flower appear in summer. Given a leafy, lime-free soil, this choice woodlander would be an unusual, though much more expensive, alternative to the tellima as a companion for red witch hazels.

The narrow, grassy, dark green blades of lilyturf, *Liriope muscari*, form an interesting textural contrast with broad leaves, and with their tussocky habit of growth to a height of 8in or more are capable of making similarly dense cover. In the fall, grape hyacinth-like spikes of bright mauve flowers like shiny beads appear. 'Monroe's White' has white flowers. It is worth going over the plants with shears in spring to rid them of the old, winter-tatty leaves and encourage fresh growth.

For a spongy film of green over the soil in places that are cool but not too dark there is *Arenaria balearica*, and even the dreaded *Soleirolia soleirolii* (syn. *Helxine soleirolii*) has its place as a dense green carpet among shrubs, as long as you never allow it near small plants. Even then you may have to tear it out in handfuls to keep it under control. The better-behaved leptinellas (formerly *Cotula*) make dense, flat mats resembling tiny ferns. *Leptinella squalida* is bronze in leaf and bears creamy button flowers, while the slightly larger *L. potentillina* is green.

Most of the other evergreen perennials recommended as ground-cover, though useful, lack the visual substance and unfussy unity of these few. Furthermore, they may also be less efficient as weed-excluders, for some of them grow bare at the center as they spread in search of new territory, thus allowing weeds to infiltrate. For this reason I regard plants such as the small lamiums, *Tellima grandiflora*

and the tiarellas, *Viola labradorica* and *Cardamine trifolia*, ajugas, the mossy saxifrages and London pride as belonging among plants that create the decor of the garden rather than its framework.

Most conifers prefer an open position, but the green yews, *Taxus baccata*, grow well in shade. The spreading 'Repandens' grows slowly into a dense, dark green cover no more than 1½ft in height and about 3ft wide. Another very shade-tolerant conifer is the Pfitzer juniper, *Juniperus × media* 'Pfitzeriana,' with wide-spreading branches growing at an angle of 45 degrees and clad with drooping, feathery branchlets of soft green foliage. There are few more tolerant plants than this juniper; equally happy in sun, it can form a link between black shade and full light. Its angled branches would contrast attractively with a weeping cherry and the tabular growth of *Viburnum plicatum* 'Mariesii' to make a bold planting needing plenty of space. If these spreading junipers do outgrow their welcome, they can be cut back–but not, please, by clipping. Trace back individual branches to a suitable fork, and remove the longer branch at this point. This treatment preserves the characteristic outline of the plant, though it is better to allow enough space for plants to grow freely if you can.

On acid soils several lowly ericaceous shrubs will perform the dual role of excluding weeds and unifying disparate plantings. As well as the wintergreen, *Gaultheria procumbens*, there is the cowberry, *Vaccinium vitis-idaea*, which also bears showy red fruits, and its cultivar 'Koralle.' The cranberry, *V. oxycoccus*, and the American cranberry, *V. macrocarpon*, grow closer to the ground, their tiny leaves making good cover for the moist, leafy soil they relish. If you grow them among rhododendrons take care not to allow the little carpets to grow over and into the rhododendrons' rootballs.

Leucothoë keiskei (see page 121) has a larger counterpart in *L. fontanesiana*, with pointed, polished foliage turning to copper in winter, and white urn-shaped flowers hanging from arching stems in spring. Its variegated cultivar 'Rainbow,' with leaves marbled with pink, cream and yellow, is striking as a single plant but too jazzy to use in numbers as a quietly unifying planting.

Mahonia aquifolium
When it was first introduced to cultivation in Europe in 1823, the Oregon grape was a rich man's plant, selling for $15 each (equivalent to about three months' wages for a qualified gardener). Within 15 years it was down to 40¢ a plant, and just before the 1914 war broke out small plants could be bought for $2.25 per thousand. That made it cheap enough to plant for evergreen game coverts; no doubt the pheasants enjoyed the berries, from which a jelly just like blackcurrant can be made.

ABOVE *A regularly spaced pattern of ferns amid a close carpet of Pachysandra terminalis sets off the slim white trunks of birches and the dark yew tree beyond. Once the rather slow-growing pachysandra has established, this would be a minimum-care planting needing little more than for dead fern fronds to be cut cleanly away.*

Though it has nothing to do with the Ericaceae, *Pachysandra terminalis* is happiest in light, lime-free soil in shade, even under trees, where it quickly spreads to make a carpet of bright green, with toothed leaves clustering at the tips of the stems.

For lime soils, the merits of *Mahonia nervosa* have already been described (see page 45). To this can be added the best of the taller, faster-growing *M. aquifolium*, the Oregon grape, such as 'Smaragd' with glossy green leaves bronzing in winter, and 'Apollo' with fine clusters of bright yellow flowers in spring. Ivies, of course, will grow almost anywhere; for our purposes, cultivars of *Hedera helix* with neat, green foliage and close growth, such as 'Très Coupé,'

'Shamrock' or 'Ivalace,' would be a good choice. They are unlikely to outgrow their place even in the smallest garden. For larger spaces there is the Persian ivy, *H. colchica*, or for really broad acres the massive, non-climbing *H. hibernica* or Irish ivy.

The low and spreading cultivars of *Prunus laurocerasus*, 'Otto Luyken,' with upright stems set with narrow leaves, and 'Zabeliana,' which grows near-horizontally in great fans of slender stems and leaves, have no fads about soil, coping even with sticky clay. Though much smaller, their leaves have the same polished surface as those of the typical cherry laurel. 'Zabeliana' quickly grows to considerable width, and is suitable only for larger gardens.

Ferns

Ferns bridge the divide between framework and decor. Beautiful enough to merit close inspection or to be grown in their own special fernery (which would qualify them as collectibles), they add a lightness of touch, a grace and elegance that make them indispensable in the shady garden.

Some even qualify as ground-cover: the small creeping fern *Blechnum penna-marina* makes a dense carpet in moist, preferably lime-free soils. It can also co-exist delightfully with *Cyclamen hederifolium*, whose marbled leaves pop up when the fern is at its least effective. For alkaline soils there is the hart's tongue fern, with evergreen fronds formed of simple straps of shining green.

In the chapter on key plants (see page 112) I attempt to choose the ferns I could not be without in a shady garden. Once you succumb to their allure you will certainly want others. They all do best in leafy, open soil: heavy clay or hungry alkaline soils are unsuitable, and so are hot or windswept places, which burn the fronds.

In really wet soils the ostrich plume fern, *Matteuccia struthiopteris*, the royal fern, *Osmunda regalis*, and the sensitive fern, *Onoclea sensibilis*, all do well, as does the marsh fern, *Thelypteris palustris*, at a lower level, a modest thing compared with the splendor of the other waterside ferns.

Propagating ferns

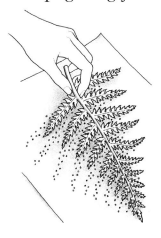

Fern spores are normally ripe in late summer or early fall; fine as powder and brown in color, they are easily blown away. Collect them by simply holding a sheet of paper beneath the frond, tapping it, and folding the paper carefully around the captive spores.

Sow the spores at once, or store them dry in a refrigerator until late winter. Fill a pot or a tray with moist sphagnum peat squeezed dry of surplus water. Dust the spores onto the peat, cover with clear plastic or glass and put it in a shaded place under cover or indoors.

The only reasonably drought-tolerant ferns are the male fern, *Dryopteris filix-mas*, and the golden-scaled male fern, *D. affinis*, the common polypody, *Polypodium vulgare*, and the soft shield fern, *Polystichum setiferum*. I would not, however, risk any of the choice polystichums except in ideal soil and conditions.

In really warm, sheltered shade, the tree ferns add a sense of prehistory, with their shaggy trunks and great fronds spreading overhead. Caught by the shafts of sunlight penetrating the tree canopy overhead, they reveal their fine tracery. The least frost-tender is probably *Dicksonia antarctica*; if this thrives for you, you could try *D. fibrosa* and *D. squarrosa* with golden-brown and near-black trunks respectively, though they are reckoned to be distinctly less hardy. Frost-free conditions are also needed for the cyatheas, of which the most likely to stand a degree or two of frost is *Cyathea dealbata*, the silver tree fern; others are *C. cooperi* and the black tree fern, *C. medullaris*, so called because of the black fur covering the rachis of the fronds. As the stem develops, all of these will themselves shelter small shade plants beneath their fronds.

The sword fern, *Nephrolepis cordifolia*, is also for frost-free climates, but the holly ferns, *Polystichum falcatum* and *P. fortunei* (syn. *Cyrtomium falcatum* and syn. *C. fortunei*), will stand a few degrees of frost. They have shining evergreen fronds of bolder outline than the usual lacy-fine fern frond.

All ferns deserve to be spared visual competition with other plants of similar height, and those that form clumps look their best as single crowns rising out of moss or fallen leaves. Once side crowns form, their characteristic shuttlecock outline becomes blurred. It is better to detach the side crowns, with their roots, and plant them elsewhere.

Many ferns can be increased by division in this way or by dividing running roots, as with any herbaceous plant. *Cystopteris bulbifera* is unusual in bearing bulbils beneath the fronds. You can space them out on sphagnum peat in seed trays to grow on until they are large enough to fend for themselves.

Instead of seeds, ferns bear spores on the backs of their fronds. These spores germinate to produce tiny plants resembling a liverwort, known as prothalli. The prothalli give rise in turn to fern "seedlings."

Ferns often sow themselves in mossy banks, on old tree stumps, between paving stones or in the crevices of shady walls: wherever they find shade and moisture. The tougher hart's tongue fern (*Phyllitis scolopendrium*) and common polypody may even sow themselves in dry walls. Small ferns such as the maidenhair and black spleenworts (*Asplenium trichomanes* and *A. adiantum-nigrum*) and the ric-rac fern, *Ceterach officinarum*, also do well in dry walls. The ric-rac fern shrivels in dry weather, and looks completely dead, but recovers with the rains, expanding again to show its green, russet-backed fronds.

Soon the prothalli will form, and next the tiny true fronds. When these are large enough to handle, separate them and prick them out into pots or trays of sphagnum peat until they have grown large enough to plant. Keep them moist and out of drying winds, especially while they are still small.

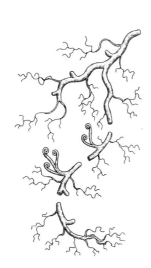

Ferns that have running roots, such as the ostrich plume fern, Matteuccia struthiopteris, *the oak fern,* Gymnocarpium dryopteris, *beech fern,* Phegopteris connectilis, *and the sensitive fern,* Onoclea sensibilis, *and many others, can be increased by division, best done in early fall or very early spring.*

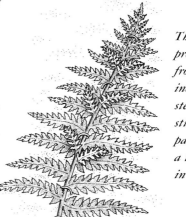

The polystichums produce buds along their fronds, and can be increased by pinning the stems down, either while still attached to the parent or, detached, into a tray of sphagnum peat in a closed frame.

THE DÉCOR

Just as a room gains character from the finishing touches—a picture on the wall, a family photograph, a shelf of books—so a garden is completed and personalized with the transient effects of flowers and the seasonal changes of deciduous leaves.

Shade plants offer elegance rather than brilliance in the main, fine drawing rather than full-brush color. Even sweeps of color are often restful compared with the flowers of the sunny garden.

Shade plants lend themselves to broad effects as well as to fine detail. Here the dinner plate-sized leaves of Astilboides tabularis *(syn.* Rodgersia tabularis*), which retain their spring-fresh coloring all summer, contrast with the tiny flowers of* Claytonia sibirica *(syn.* Montia sibirica*) in a weed-excluding planting beneath trees.*

Borders in shade

ABOVE *A wide planting of* Hosta montana *'Aureomarginata' and a single* H. sieboldiana elegans *are set with a generous group of* Iris sibirica, *and bare soil is quickly hidden by* Vinca minor *'Argenteovariegata.* OPPOSITE *The lacy foliage of dicentras echoes the silvery fronds of the Japanese painted fern,* Athyrium niponicum pictum, *and the bold shuttlecocks of a* Dryopteris. *There are flowers too in this shady border: lily of the valley, (*Convallaria*), the red and green double* Aquilegia *'Nora Barlow,' as well as the pink and white lockets of dicentras.*

You can make a border of flowering and foliage plants just as well in shade as in sun, of course: it will simply have a different character. There will probably be more beautiful leaves than in a conventional flower border; but there can also be plenty of flowers in a shady border.

One of the most popular herbaceous perennials grown for its foliage in shaded borders is the hosta, of which a selection is described in the chapter on key plants (see page 114). There are green, gold, blue and variegated hostas in many leaf sizes, from little more than a thumbnail to larger than a dinner plate; some have handsome flowers as well. Although some are slow-growing, most of the larger ones increase reasonably quickly in rich, moist soil. Once you have a fair-sized clump, you can make new plantings by cutting out wedges, as described in the later chapter, through the seasons (see page 103). One or two slices out of an established clump will make hardly any difference to it even in the first year; and the wedges go to make new plantings or to increase the size of the original group. Even in a small garden the occasional wide planting of bold foliage may be needed to give a sense of unity and restfulness.

Hostas' usually broad, always undivided leaf blades contrast well with ferns, with the dissected leaves of dicentras and astilbes, or with the swords of Siberian iris; and all of these plants, bar the ferns, have beautiful flowers as well as good foliage. Fine foliage also belongs to the veratrums, whose great pleated, poisonous leaves are topped by spires of flower, maroon-black in *Veratrum nigrum*, alabaster white in *V. album*. *Smilacina racemosa*, a relative of Solomon's seal, tops its arching stems with a small spire of fluffy, fragrant, ivory flowers in spring. Species peonies such as *Paeonia obovata alba*, the even more beautiful lemon-white *P. obovata willmottiae* and 'Mollie the witch,' *P. mlokosewitchii*, have cupped flowers enhanced by round-lobed foliage unfolding in tones of dusky pink and dove gray. Most peonies have colored spring foliage that is the perfect setting for small daffodils. Even though their flowers are fleeting, their elegance, and the bonus of good leaves, makes them worth space in small gardens.

Alchemilla mollis, for all its invasively free-seeding tendencies, is an invaluable flower-and-foliage plant for shade, with pleated, rounded, velvet-soft leaves holding dewdrops at their hearts and strung along their margins, and hazy chartreuse-green flowers in early summer. Cut the whole plant to the ground as it fades, flower and leaf alike, water well, and you need wait almost no time for fresh new leaves to grow. This is especially important in small gardens, because if the flowers are left too long, seedlings may take over the whole garden.

Although most begonias are frost-tender, one species will stand quite severe cold, disappearing below ground during winter. *Begonia grandis evansiana* has typically lopsided, bold foliage of succulent texture, wine-red on the reverse, and nodding pink or white flowers opening from tinted buds in summer and fall. In sheltered shade, it grows lush and reaches at least 1ft. It forms bulbils which you can save, setting them in trays of potting compost to grow on until they have formed new plants large enough to fend for themselves in the open garden.

Plenty of shade-bearing perennials chosen above all for their flowers also have handsome foliage. Monkshoods (*Aconitum* species) bear their sulky blue or ivory helmets over deeply cut, polished leaves; most heucheras have attractively marbled leaves; and the cimicifugas hold their white spires over a base of dissected foliage. The balance of flower and foliage reaches its apotheosis in *Kirengeshoma palmata*, a Japanese perennial with leaves like a plane or a tulip tree's, dark stems, and waxy shuttlecock flowers of soft primrose in the fall.

Almost all the components of the flower border in shade do better, in fact, than the usual dull foliage offerings of conventional border flowers such as Michaelmas daisies or heleniums. The hardy geraniums range from the green, dissected leaf of *Geranium clarkei* 'Kashmir White' to the round, figured-velvet grayness of *G. renardii*; Japanese anemones, *Anemone hupehensis*, have vine-like leaves and are stout enough to hold their own among large shrubs, while *A. × lesseri*, which has vivid magenta-pink flowers, or quiet *A. rivularis*, in white backed with blue, echo them in miniature.

Astrantia major, the masterwort, has divided leaves below its ivory-green, pincushion flower-heads; *A. maxima* is finer in flower, with dusky pink pincushions and leaves like a Lenten rose. If you like these slightly off beat colors, plant *A. maxima* in a group which will give interest from spring onwards, with *Dicentra formosa* 'Stuart Boothman,' pink columbines and the pink cow parsley (*Chaerophyllum hirsutum* 'Roseum'), *Polemonium reptans* 'Lambrook Mauve,' *Geranium macrorrhizum* 'Bevan's Variety' in magenta-crimson, and pink Spanish bluebells (*Hyacinthoides hispanica*). The backdrop could be a shrub with variegated foliage, and for still more flower color you might plant a mauve-pink clematis like 'Nelly Moser,' which is surprisingly shade-tolerant, to twine through the branches of the shrub. Overhead, the early, pale foliage of *Amelanchier arborea* would enhance the pinkish tones, and in the fall the red-purple fruits would appear amid the now orange-red foliage.

Shade-loving plants with variegated leaves

Plants with variegated leaves make a point of drawing your attention away from the flowers. In shade, white or cream variegations bring a light touch which is the rough equivalent visually of silver-leaved plants in full sun, while yellow markings resemble dappled sunlight in the shadows. If you appreciate these effects there is more to choose from than the vast range of hostas, which offer every conceivable permutation of green, cream, ivory, yellow and white. Variegations can become addictive, but used with discretion and kept away from the wilder corners, they have their own special value in the shady garden.

There is a variegated astrantia, 'Sunningdale Variegated,' with bold primrose splashes on the leaf lobes, fading towards green as summer advances. A few geraniums have sported variegations: *Geranium macrorrhizum* 'Variegatum,' *G.* × *monacense* 'Muldoon,' and the mourning widow, *G. phaeum.* Both variegated *Brunnera macrophylla*, 'Dawson's White' and 'Hadspen Cream,' are no less pretty than the plain green when bearing their forget-me-not sprays, and have more to offer than weed-exclusion thereafter. The prettiest of the comfreys, *Symphytum caucasicum*, with sky-blue tubular bells, is green leaved but 'Goldsmith' has green and yellow foliage, and the splendid *S. uplandicum* 'Variegatum' has boldly cream-splashed leaves, at their best later in summer.

Of the two variegated phloxes I know, one, *P. paniculata* 'Norah Leigh,' has a weak constitution but is exceptionally pretty with pale lilac flowers, while 'Harlequin' is more assertive, with cream and green leaves below bright purple flowers. The boldness of *Persicaria* (Tovara) *virginiana* 'Painter's Palette' is all in the foliage, decorated with primrose splashes and a chevron of mahogany at mid-leaf.

Variegated grasses, such as *Holcus mollis* 'Albo-variegatus' and *Molinia caerulea* 'Variegata,' or the taller and busily invasive gardener's garters, *Phalaris arundinacea picta* 'Picta,' or pink-flushed *Glyceria maxima* 'Variegata,' bring the same lightness of touch with contrasting form: the holcus, especially, is almost wholly white at first. *Milium effusum aureum* is a soft-bladed grass seeding true, its pale gold infants soon making a carpet or, with maturity, standing out among darker leaves and bursting into a delicate fountain of citron sprays when in flower. With sharp-toned daffodils for spring and spurges (*Euphorbia*) for later, it makes a lime-yellow harmony beneath *Gleditsia triacanthos* 'Sunburst.' *Hakonechloa macra* 'Aureola' is possibly the finest grass for shade. Its gracefully arching, yellow- and green-striped leaves turn a reddish color in the fall.

There are a handful of deciduous shrubs with variegated or golden leaves that can add greatly to the garden decor in summer. The shrubby dogwood, *Cornus alba*, comes in several variants, from the white-splashed *C. alba* 'Elegantissima' (an ideal host to *Clematis* 'Nelly Moser' in the pink-toned scheme on page 61) and green-and-gold *C. alba* 'Spaethii,' to the soft lemon-green *C. alba* 'Aurea.' These shrubby dogwoods are also grown for their brightly colored winter stems: to keep them at their best, cut all the branches to near ground-level in late winter.

Just as undemanding are the elders, *Sambucus nigra*: 'Marginata' and 'Aureomarginata' are bordered with ivory and primrose respectively, while 'Pulverulenta' looks as though it has had a flour-bag thrown over it. 'Aurea' is all gold, and coarser than *S. racemosa* 'Plumosa Aurea,' which has dissected leaves touched with bronze in spring. These too are kept compact and produce their best foliage if cut hard back at the end of each winter. If you have room for only one, make it *S. racemosa* 'Plumosa Aurea.'

The variegated mock orange, *Philadelphus coronarius* 'Bowles' Variety,' is pale and charming, with fragrant cream blossoms in summer; it is a restrained shrub unlikely to outgrow its welcome in a small space. There is a golden mock orange too, *P. coronarius* 'Aureus,' larger in growth than its variegated counterpart, and a golden weigela, *Weigela* 'Looymansii Aurea,' which does itself no service by

bearing pink flowers but can be most effective once these have fallen. The same lack of color awareness briefly spoils the slow-growing, chartreuse-leaved *Ribes sanguineum* 'Brocklebankii' in spring. *Physocarpus opulifolius* 'Luteus,' on the other hand, bears only insignificant whitish flowers, with leaves which are touched with bronze as they unfurl in spring. The golden Guelder rose, *Viburnum opulus* 'Aureum,' has modest lacecap flowers. Any of these golden shrubs could host a blue *Clematis alpina*, though the ribes, even in maturity, might risk being overwhelmed.

BELOW *The bold white edging of the dark, gleaming leaves of* Hosta crispula *is echoed by flights of pure white buttercups over glossy, dissected leaves of* Ranunculus aconitifolius.

Silvers and grays for shady places

If you wanted to design an all-white planting for a shady garden, you would have to forgo almost all the silver-leaved plants that add their version of non-color to more traditional white gardens in full light. There are just a few gray-leaved plants that do well in bright shade, however; they would be invaluable as linking plants if you have a border that passes from sun to shade and in which you want to avoid abrupt transitions.

Several evergreen shrubs belong in this category, the pewter-gray *Olearia macrodonta* and silver-backed *Elaeagnus macrophylla* among them. Both are for reasonably mild areas. The deciduous *Rosa glauca* fades from plum-purple to dove-gray in shade, and at a lower level so does *Fuchsia magellanica* 'Versicolor,' losing most of the pink tones that suffuse its leaves in full light. If you emulate the pink scheme on page 61 in a section of border which is partly sunny, these would be the perfect shrubs to bridge the transition from shade to sun.

Graceful willows such as the rosemary-leaved *Salix elaeagnos*, its needles gray above and white beneath, and tall, slender *S. exigua*, do well in light shade. Neither of these is a shrub for small gardens. Although it can become fairly large, *Rubus cockburnianus* is so good as a four-season shrub that it might well earn a place. It has arching, pendulous stems, which are waxy and vivid white, and small, purple flowers in early summer. The leaves, which are green above, have white, felt-like undersides. Cut out the oldest stems each year to maintain the fountain of white stems that is its best winter effect.

LEFT *Silver-leaved plants are usually associated with sunny places, but perennials can bring a silvery touch to cooler corners too. A pineapple-flowered* Eucomis *is the greenest thing in this planting which includes* Hosta sieboldiana elegans, *the narrow, arching, platinum-blotched leaves of* Pulmonaria longifolia, *and a white-variegated form of* Euonymus fortunei.

RIGHT *This cool-toned planting is composed of the silver-gray painted fern,* Athyrium niponicum pictum, *the blue-leaved* Hosta *'Halcyon,' a crested polypody, an arching stem of cream-striped Solomon's seal,* Polygonatum × hybridum *'Striatum' and the toothed, three-parted leaves of* Helleborus lividus.

The silvery-gray perennial anaphalis actually prefer a moisture-retentive soil and are happy in light shade. Their white-felted stems and white everlasting flowers in late summer enhance their paleness. *Anaphalis triplinervis* has three-veined leaves on 1ft stems; *A. cinnamomea* is taller, with leaves very white-felted beneath, and the similar *A. margaritacea* has narrower leaves.

The tall stems of *Lysimachia ephemerum*, reaching 3ft or so, are set with narrow, smooth, gray leaves and slender spikes of pewter-white flowers in sum-mer, making a strongly vertical note in contrast to blue-gray hostas, for example. A different treatment would pair two verticals of differing colors: the cool lysimachia with bright magenta loosestrife, *Lythrum salicaria*. Moist soil suits these best.

The forms of pulmonaria with heavily silvered leaves, like their greener counterparts, prefer a shaded place, as do the cultivars of *Lamium maculatum*, 'Beacon Silver' with rose-pink flowers and 'White Nancy' with white, in which the silver stripe extends across the whole leaf.

Two color ranges for a shady border

The groups proposed here comprise plants that are not hard to grow in any reasonable garden soil in light or part-shade: at the foot of a high wall, for example, or in the shadow of distant, not overhanging trees. Plant them in generous groups; long drifts generally look better than blobby blocks, as gaps show up less obviously.

The two basic color ranges are those from the blue half of the spectrum, and from the yellow. It is perfectly possible to link the two color ranges, especially if you stick to the softer shades of mauve-pink-purple and of lemon, lime and cream, not just for the linking group but also for the main planting. These paler tones show up well in shade, though it can be fun to inject some bright color, for example the strong mauve of the astilbe in the group below, or the brilliant yellow daisies of *Rudbeckia fulgida* 'Goldsturm,' enhanced by their black central cone.

Left to right: blue spectrum–*Anemone hupehensis* 'September Charm,' *Astilbe chinensis taquetii* 'Superba,' *Hosta sieboldiana, Rosa glauca* (at back); **linking group** –*Hemerocallis* 'Marion Vaughn,' *Phlox paniculata, Hosta ventricosa* 'Aureomarginata'; **yellow spectrum**– *Nepeta govaniana, Alchemilla mollis, Hosta helonioides albopicta, Osmanthus decorus* (at back).

Blue spectrum

All the plants here flower in pink, mauve, lilac, purple or crimson, and have blue-green rather than yellow-green leaves. White flowers also belong here, especially if faintly blushed with pink or mauve. This group would look well in the same field of vision as a pink Japanese cherry or *Amelanchier arborea.* There are plenty of other plants you could use to extend the same color range to other seasons, including *Aquilegia vulgaris* 'Nivea,' a tall columbine with white flowers and gray leaves, and the pink cowparsley, *Chaerophyllum hirsutum* 'Roseum,' pink dicentras such as *D. formosa* 'Stuart Boothman' with pewter-gray foliage and bright pink lockets, and the garnet-red *Astrantia carniolica rubra*, with its pincushion flowers. To carpet the ground between drifts of these, add *Lamium maculatum* 'Beacon Silver' for its silvered leaves and magenta-pink dead-nettle flowers.

Anemone hupehensis 'September Charm': flowers with many narrow, soft lilac-pink petals in early fall.

Astilbe chinensis taquetii 'Superba': good dark crinkled and dissected foliage; slender spires of strong mauve flowers in late summer.

Hosta sieboldiana elegans: large, puckered glaucous-blue leaves.

Rosa glauca: foliage plum-flushed in sun, pewter-gray in shade; small bright pink flowers followed by red hips if unpruned, finest foliage if hard-pruned in spring.

Linking group

The group at the center of this border joins
the mauve-pink-purple colors with the
yellows and greens with a partnership of bold
shapes and soft, cool tones.
Hosta ventricosa 'Aureomarginata': heart-shaped
leaves which have an irregular, yellowish
margin and mauve flowers.
Hemerocallis 'Marion Vaughn': cool lemon day
lily with fragrant blooms.
Phlox paniculata: tall, airy, lavender-mauve
panicles of flowers.

Yellow spectrum

Choose plants with green or lime-yellow
foliage and flowers of all the shades of yellow,
from cream and primrose to ocher and
chartreuse. An appropriate setting would be
the strong greens of yew, osmanthus or
Choisya ternata. The seasonal interest could be
extended with daisy-flowered doronicums and
acid-green euphorbias for spring, and pale
yellow *Aconitum* 'Ivorine' or the yellow
foxglove (*Digitalis grandiflora*) for early
summer.

Alchemilla mollis: rounded, soft green leaves
and sprays of lime-green flowers in summer.
Hosta rohdeifolia albopicta: narrow oblong
leaves with broad cream margins; lilac
flowers.
Nepeta govaniana: shade-loving catmint
relative with airy sprays of primrose flowers
on 3ft stems over pale green leaves.
Osmanthus decorus: broad-domed shrub up to
10ft tall, with bold, glossy, dark evergreen
leaves; white, fragrant flowers in spring.

Flowering shrubs as décor

ABOVE *Mophead hydrangeas look quite at home in formal settings, as here, where a gravel path to a wrought-iron gate overhung with cherry laurel is flanked by hydrangea-filled box-edged beds. These clear pink shades occur in hydrangeas where there is some lime in the soil.*

Some shrubs whose main contribution is their flowers also form part of the décor of the garden. The familiar mophead and lacecap hydrangeas, for example, are good at one thing only: flowers, and plenty of them, for three or four months of the year. Generally I would keep the mopheads, with their domesticated appearance, near the house or the more formal parts of the garden, and use the more graceful lacecaps among other shrubs or in a woodland setting. Most are fairly expansive shrubs, but a few, as noted in the selection that follows, are especially suitable for small gardens.

There are many cultivars of *Hydrangea macrophylla*, in both lacecap and mophead form. Lime soils make for pink hydrangeas, acid for blue; on neutral soil, with a pH of around 6.5, you are apt to get rather indeterminate mauves, but a light dressing of lime will turn them pink. It is a little harder to "blue" hydrangeas from mauve than to make them pink, but a scattering of aluminium sulphate well watered in among the stems in late fall should do the trick. Use about 1lb for a fair-sized bush. Further encouragement can be given by watering at two week intervals in spring with a solution of Epsom salts (magnesium sulphate) at a rate of about 2oz per 2 gallons per bush.

The lacecaps usually come in white or blue/pink. Exceptionally, *Hydrangea* 'Geoffrey Chadbund' has deep red lacecap flowers, with the best color given by plants in neutral or just limy soil; if yours is acid and the color is tainted with purple, add a dash of lime to the soil to steer it towards the desired cherry red. The lacecap cultivars of *H. serrata* are hardier, smaller and therefore among the best for limited spaces, and happiest in shade; again, they come in blue/pink. There are two delicious cultivars that begin white and age through pink to crimson, regardless of soil pH: 'Rosalba' and 'Grayswood.' 'Preziosa' is a neat and compact mophead cultivar or hybrid of *H. serrata* which opens clear pink and matures to deep crimson; and where the sun strikes its leaves, they too are reddened. It is ideal as a component of the dusky pink groups already suggested (see pages 61 and 66). One of the most appealing for the shady garden is *H. involucrata* 'Hortensis,' a small shrub with frothy double, creamy pink flowers in summer and early fall.

The snowball trees, *Viburnum opulus* 'Roseum' and the more refined *V. plicatum*, flower with equal abandon in light shade or in sun. I am inclined to regard the lacecap forms of *V. plicatum* as more than décor, for with their habit of growth they have great character. They also need plenty of room to develop this characteristic outline: it is a waste to try to cram them into small spaces.

The common elder, *Sambucus nigra*, is invaluable for really rough corners, and decorative when covered in its creamy, frothy blossom, but too big for most gardens. Given the space, it is worth keeping a bush, for a supply of the muscat-scented flowers to add to gooseberry pie or for elderflower "champagne," and of the black fruits for wine or elderberry rob, a cordial for sore throats in winter. As well as the colored foliage forms described on page 38, the elder has a most garden-worthy selection in *S. nigra* 'Laciniata,' with finely cut leaves and flowers of the same ivory abundance. The very slow-growing selec-

tion of *S. racemosa* known as 'Tenuifolia' has leaves as dissected as a cut-leaved maple, which it also rather resembles in its humpy, mushroom silhouette: a choice little shrub to harmonize with small shade-loving plants, and more tolerant of alkaline or dryish soils than true Japanese maples.

The decorative value of a shrub may lie more in its fruits than its flowers. *Decaisnea fargesii* is a tallish shrub with pinnate foliage, and sprays of delicate chartreuse-yellow bells that merit close inspection, but the fruits are astonishing: shaped like broad bean pods, they are indigo-blue in color.

ABOVE *The lacecap hydrangeas such as this pale blue* Hydrangea macrophylla *have a more informal air than the mopheads opposite, so they are ideally suited to relaxed plantings of shrubs and other shade-lovers. At the heart of the flowerhead are the deeper blue, fertile florets.*

69

RIGHT *Deciduous azaleas decorate a woodland garden in spring with their dancing flowers: their soft tones—cream opening from pink-tipped buds and pink with a discreet orange flare—blend with the bluebells that spread a generous carpet among the azalea stems. Many azaleas include fragrance, or flaming fall tints, or both, among their attributes.*

Decorative shrubs for acid soils

The lime-hating *Enkianthus campanulatus* also develops a layered outline as it matures, but this is an open, elegant shrub with none of the muscularity of the snowball or lacecap viburnums. The small cream bells, striped with terra-cotta, hang in clusters from the branches in late spring, and the neat leaves flare into woodfire colors in the fall. There is a white-flowered form, *E. campanulatus albiflorus*, and a red, *E. campanulatus palibinii*. In time the shrub may reach 10ft and can be pruned to make a little tree. The smaller *E. cernuus rubens* has deep brick-red flowers and vivid fall color. They bring a lightness of touch to plantings of rhododendrons, and their flower colors are in harmony with the sharp yellow young leaves of oaks. Although *E. campanulatus* in particular can grow tall, it is slender enough to tuck into small gardens.

The fothergillas, also acid-lovers, are less dainty, but their fuzzy bottlebrushes of fragrant cream flowers in spring are a pretty accompaniment to red rhododendrons, and their fall color is a warm yellow or orange-scarlet. The taller *Fothergilla major* includes the Monticola Group, which used to be a separate species; *F. gardenii* is more compact. *F. gardenii* 'Blue Mist,' a new introduction, looks promising, with its young foliage emerging (after the flowers have faded) in a surprising shade of powder blue, and maturing to blue-green.

The bloom on the leaves of *Zenobia pulverulenta* is almost white, and in early summer the flowers are pure white bells, much larger than those of the enkianthuses, like a magnified lily-of-the-valley, though without the sweet perfume. To keep the foliage in tip-top condition, cut the branches back as soon as the bells fade. This also keeps the shrub compact, ideal for a small garden.

Deciduous azaleas are décor *par excellence*, of course, with their butterfly blooms in a range of bright, pure or gentle colors. The Piedmont azalea, *Rhododendron canascens*, covers itself with innumerable small, white-pink to rose, powerfully fragrant flowers in spring, and fires up in the fall as the leaves die. It is a big shrub, reaching 10ft high and as much wide. It coincides in flower with the earliest of the

OPPOSITE *Mixing deciduous azaleas and rhododendrons can be hazardous, as their color ranges—predominantly yellow, orange and scarlet for the azaleas, pink to lilac and purple for the rhododendrons—may clash. But here Rhododendron 'Naomi' towers over pink-flowered evergreen azaleas in a harmonious grouping with plenty of emollient green.*

hybrid deciduous azaleas, the Mollis group, characterized by many shades of yellow from straw to lemon to saffron, with some bright terra-cotta and ember reds, as well as salmon- and rose-pinks, often with an orange flare.

In a large garden sweeps of these, with the emphasis on the yellows, make a fine picture with yellow Welsh poppies, English bluebells, forget-me-nots and wild yellow violets such as *Viola glabella* and *V. pensylvanica*, among the white stems of birches or beneath white-flowering cherries.

If you prefer pink azaleas, and have the space for them, the season opens with *Rhododendron albrechtii*, a shrub of 8ft with deep rose-pink flowers, and the taller *R. schlippenbachii*, with fragrant flowers in shades from pale pink to soft rose. Later comes *R. vaseyi*, with shell-pink, rose-flecked flowers and vivid fall leaf. Match them, again, with white-stemmed birches, or float the snowy blossom of *Amelanchier canadensis* among and over them, and encourage lily-of-the-valley or the diminutive *Cornus canadensis*, with its tiny dogwood leaves and flowers on 6in stems, to spread beneath—but only if your garden is reasonably large.

Later azaleas, the Ghents, Knaphill and Exbury hybrids, derive from the vivid scarlet *Rhododendron calendulaceum* and tree-like, white-flowered, scented *R. arborescens*, the spice-scented swamp honeysuckle, *R. viscosum*, and the very late-flowering *R. prunifolium* in brilliant orange-red.

At a much lower level, there are the half-evergreen azaleas with the blood of *R. kaempferi*, tending to soft bricky pinks and terra-cotta; 'Daimio' and 'Mikado' are two good, late-flowering selections. Evergreen azaleas proper almost qualify as shrubs for the framework of the garden, whether large or small, for though a stark white such as 'Palestrina' or the incredibly shade-tolerant *R. mucronatum* may be chosen primarily for their flowers, some develop a bold, tiered quality that has great character at all times. This is especially true of the searing magenta 'Amoenum' and crimson 'Amoenum Coccineum.'

The pretty highbush blueberries, *Vaccinium corymbosum*, rival the brightest azaleas with their fall colors, and if you are prepared to fling a net over them you can enjoy the delicious fruits as well.

Using bulbs and climbers

In nature, plants in a mature community grow in layers. Beneath the tree canopy you are likely to find a shrubby layer, and below that a herbaceous layer. In the same ground space there may well also be plants which appear for only a short season above the soil, spending much of their annual cycle in a state of dormancy, with their energies held in storage organs such as bulbs or tubers. And yet another layer is added by climbers, opportunistic plants that use a shrub or tree to hoist themselves upwards.

Gardeners have long exploited these natural tendencies in order to coax twice or three times the value from the same piece of ground. It is a style of planting that is well adapted to shade gardening. You need to choose the plants carefully, of course. It is no good planting bulbs that need a serious summer baking in cool, leafy soil where the sun will hardly reach them after the trees above have leafed up.

In the mauve, pink and glaucous groups proposed on page 61, you could plant a drift of the Spanish bluebell, *Hyacinthoides hispanica*, which bears its soft blue, mauve-pink or white flowers in spring on 1ft stems. Also happy in light shade is *Anemone blanda*, which has many-petaled flowers of lavender-blue, white, pink 'Charmer' or perhaps the potent magenta, white-eyed 'Radar.'

Although gladioli are regarded as sun-lovers, *Gladiolus communis byzantinus* flowers freely in light shade, and spreads fast in light soil. The magenta-purple butterfly blooms are held on 3ft stems in early summer. Later in the season, in late summer and the fall, comes *G. papilio*, its hooded, muted lilac flowers marked with green and cream in the throat, and held on 4ft stems over grassy, glaucous foliage.

In the fall the colchicums, inaccurately called fall crocus, emerge naked from the soil; the leaves appear later and are glossily handsome in spring before a brief period of disgrace as they fade. Neither *Colchicum autumnale* nor the more splendid *C. speciosum* is hard to grow; both have flowers of mauve-pink or white. 'Waterlily' has flowers with many narrow, lilac-pink petals. If these do well, there are others to collect, some with darker checkering on the petals. *Liriope muscari*, with its evergreen foliage and bright mauve flower spikes in the fall, makes the ideal setting for colchicum flowers.

Among the sharper-toned groups of yellow, lime and orange, the season opens with crocuses and narcissi, many of them quite at home in lightly shaded places. There are so many different kinds of each that the choice is a matter of personal taste. My own selection would be from the cultivars of *Crocus*

Growing a climber in a host tree or shrub

When planting a climber in a tree or shrub, you need to prepare the soil carefully. To prevent the tree from stealing nutrients, line the planting hole with a bottomless box of thin boards before planting your climber. While the boards rot the climber will have a season to establish.

With deep-rooted trees you may find a space between anchoring roots close to the trunk. The soil will be dry and poor, so preparation is important, and an annual dose of fertilizer and mulch is essential.

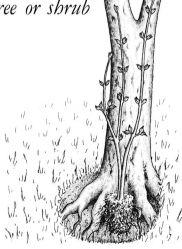

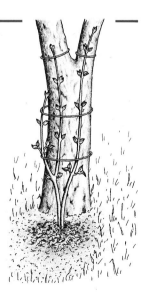

Excavate a planting hole as large as possible; avoid the host tree's roots as well as possible to minimize competition. Ideally plant the climber to windward, so that the prevailing gales will blow it more firmly into the arms of its host. Fill the hole with a rich planting mixture of compost and leafy soil.

USING BULBS AND CLIMBERS

chrysanthus, with half-height daffodils such as 'Dove Wings' in white and soft yellow, or 'Little Witch' with windswept yellow petals.

A pretty underplanting for any of the golden shrubs on page 63 would pair the purple-leaved *Viola labradorica purpurea* with golden grass, *Milium effusum aureum*, or the golden Creeping Jenny, *Lysimachia nummularia* 'Aurea'; snowdrops would flower at the turn of the year with the violet's dark foliage as a backdrop. You could add a dark clematis such as the *Clematis viticella* hybrid 'Royal Velours' for a dramatic summer effect.

Climbers can drape themselves on virtually any shrub in your border except the smallest. *Rosa glauca* could host *Clematis* 'Duchess of Albany,' with its tulip-shaped pink flowers on almost herbaceous stems, or one of the *C. viticella* hybrids which are pruned almost to the ground in winter; *C. viticella* 'Purpurea Plena Elegans' would be a good choice, on account of its soft gray-purple, double rosette flowers. Both flower as freely in light shade as in sun.

With lime-green foliage or yellow flowers the choice might be the scentless scarlet honeysuckle *Lonicera × brownii* 'Dropmore Scarlet.' Shrubs with variegated or colored leaves can be given a change of personality during the season if you use them to host

a climber. The *viticella* clematis with richly colored flowers—wine-red 'Abundance' or the brighter 'Kermesina,' violet 'Etoile Violette' or purple 'Polish Spirit'—make startling contrasts with green and white dogwoods, or Byzantine mixtures among golden or yellow-variegated leaves. In light shade their intense colors are dramatic against the bright backdrop of foliage.

ABOVE *In the fall the flowers of colchicums burst leafless from the soil. Here* Colchicum *'Glory of Heemstede' (syn. 'Conquest') is partnered by a fern,* Athyrium distentifolium.

Plant the climber with the soil surface at the same level as when it was in its pot or nursery quarters. Firm it in well and water it thoroughly. Use soft garden twine to secure its stems to the host tree.

When planting a climber beyond the reach of the host tree's feeding roots (as a rough guide the roots extend as far out as the canopy), provide a cane or stout string to lead the climber into the outer branches of the host. Otherwise the planting technique is the same.

Gardening in layers to span the seasons

Ways of using the natural growth habits of plants to pack more into the same space and to extend the season have already cropped up here and there in these pages. In the groups on page 41 some of the suggested plants are bulbs–snowdrops, martagon lilies–and others are small perennials such as primroses, which can be tucked into many a congenial corner with leafy, cool soil. They take almost no space, and the same is true of many climbers. You could jazz up a quiet green and white group with *Tropaeolum speciosum*, which bears its scarlet nasturtium flowers in summer and fall. You can also use the principle of gardening in layers to transform a one-season shrub to an all-year picture.

Extending summer interest

Several favorite shrubs are briefly handsome in spring or summer flower, but offer nothing much beyond that. Many could be arborized, as shown on page 21, to become a source of shade and support for climbers. A lilac, for example, could host and shelter the following, all in colors echoing or toning with its flowers.

Athyrium niponicum pictum: fern with divided, silvery gray fronds on maroon stems.

Anemonopsis macrophylla: nodding, lavender-blue flowers in open sprays in summer, over ferny leaves; dislikes drying winds.

Clematis 'Little Nell': a *C. viticella* hybrid with white flowers veined and margined with mauve in summer.

Cyclamen hederifolium: hardy, fall-flowering cyclamen; leaves die away at mid-summer and reappear in the fall.

Helleborus lividus: for milder climates (or substitute *H. argutifolius*); gray-marbled, toothed leaves and nodding cups of dove-gray or green, flushed pink, in early spring.

Lilium martagon cattaniae: a martagon lily of darkest maroon, flowering in early summer.

ABOVE **Left to right:** *Athyrium niponicum pictum* (front), *Anemonopsis macrophylla* (back), lilac with *Clematis* 'Little Nell,' *Cyclamen hederifolium*, *Helleborus lividus*.

Extending winter interest

The same principle applies in reverse with winter-flowering shrubs. All witch hazels, for example, bear flowers in the pale yellow to deep rust-red range, with mid-yellow the most common color; the fall foliage is yellow to orange also. Let this set the color theme for a climber and underplanting for the rest of the year, with contrasting tones of lavender-blue and ultramarine.

Anemone nemorosa 'Allenii': deepest blue wood anemone; flowers in spring; soon forms colonies of spreading rhizomes.

Cardamine raphanifolia (syn. *C. latifolia*) (lady's smock): spreading, leafy mats topped by bright lavender-purple flowers in spring.

Clematis 'Perle d'Azur': soft Wedgwood-blue flowers in summer and early fall.

Corydalis ochroleuca: ferny, gray-green foliage and spikes of alabaster-white, spurred flowers from spring to fall. *C. lutea* is similar in lemon yellow.

Hacquetia epipactis: tiny umbellifer with acid-yellow flowers in little green ruffs; should not be disturbed.

Narcissus cyclamineus: small, bright lemon flowers with backswept perianth in early spring; prefers shade and moist, acid soil.

Pulmonaria longiflora: pick of the lungworts, with long, narrow, white-spotted leaves and heads of bright ultramarine-blue flowers on 1ft stems in late spring and summer.

Uvularia grandiflora (merrybells): fresh green, narrow leaves and hanging bells of clear straw yellow on arching 1½ft stems in late spring.

BELOW **Left to right:** *Corydalis ochroleuca, Cardamine raphanifolia, Pulmonaria longiflora, Hacquetia epipactis, Uvularia grandiflora, Anemone nemorosa* 'Allenii,' *Narcissus cyclamineus*; at back, *Hamamelis mollis* with young growths of *Clematis* 'Perle d'Azur.'

Ephemerals: annuals and biennials

Ask people to name half a dozen annuals, and they will usually think of scarlet salvias, French marigolds and the like: colorful plants for sunny places. The shade garden has its annuals too, and as with shrubs and perennials they tend toward elegance and charm rather than showiness.

Even the bright *Impatiens*, though as colorful as any sun-lover, gain charm from the luminous quality of their flowers. They do extremely well even in quite dense shade; in Switzerland we use them in the sunless alleys between tall houses, and in California I have seen them used to great effect in the shadow of hotel awnings. The number of available colors is wide, and ranges from glistening white and palest pinks through to a potent magenta, and from coral to rich orange and scarlet. Although they enjoy plenty of moisture at the root, these two examples clearly show that, given shade, they do not suffer where the atmosphere is hot or dry.

Annuals such as this are fun: they can change the character of a corner of the garden for a season, without commitment. Next year you could grow, say, *Nemophila maculata*, which has glacier-white flowers marked with an indigo spot at the apex of each of the five petals. The shade-loving *Schizopetalon walkeri*, with its fragrant, fringed white flowers, would form drifts around the nemophila. The blue woodruff, *Asperula orientalis* (syn. *A. azurea setosa*), also prefers cool, lightly shaded places; its low, branching stems bear fragrant lilac-blue flowers.

The tobacco flowers do very well in shade that is not too dense. The day-awake selections that have been developed have no scent to accompany their pretty colors of lime green, crimson and pink as well as white, but the old *Nicotiana alata grandiflora*, though it folds down into khaki anonymity during the day, unfurls as dusk falls to reveal its fluted white trumpets, and to release its swooning perfume.

BELOW *Impatiens are ideal shade-garden ephemerals, growing equally well in containers or in the ground, asking only ample moisture at the root. Here a row of pink impatiens in terra-cotta pots brings color to a group of sword ferns (*Nephrolepis cordifolia*) beneath trees.*

RIGHT *In complete contrast to the formality of the ephemerals captive in their pots, opposite, these groups of peach-pink and white foxgloves and white sweet rocket (*Hesperis matronalis alba*) have sown themselves where they will beneath a weeping willow. More color comes from the blue and white saucers of* Campanula persicifolia, *a shade-tolerant bellflower which is easily raised from seed and excellent as a cut flower.*

Nicotiana sylvestris
The Indians of tropical
America cultivated and
ritually smoked tobacco
(Nicotiana tabacum)
long before the arrival of
the Europeans. However,
this Argentinian species is
purely ornamental, though
it may also contain
narcotic substances similar
to nicotine. Its long
tubular flowers are
fragrant at night in order
to attract night-flying
moths.

Where there is space for something much taller than these knee-high tobaccos, *Nicotiana sylvestris* fills the need. Forming wide rosettes of big, soft, sticky, pale green leaves that choke out weeds, it builds up to a great, head-topping spire of long white trumpets with a delicious, carrying perfume. The rather smaller, slenderer *N. langsdorfii* has no scent, but its little lime-green trumpets, the lip flaring wide around sky-blue anthers, are too charming to pass over.

These tobaccos are in fact tender perennials, surviving a few degrees of frost in the ground; if winters are not too severe you can expect them to reappear next spring, especially if you cover the roots with a thick mulch. If you need to grow them afresh each year, and have greenhouse space to shelter them in winter, they can be sown in the fall and planted out in spring. Spring-sown, they can be planted out to follow on from biennials such as foxgloves.

The common foxglove, *Digitalis purpurea*, is very much a shade plant, coloring European woodlands with its steeples of mauve-pink, spotted "gloves." For the garden, selections in white, primrose or peach-pink ('Sutton's Apricot') are preferable to the wildling, and if you care for them there are the Excelsior hybrids with their large flowers blaring at you from all around the stem, or the monstrous *D. gloxiniiflora* selections of the seedsmen.

The only way to be sure of maintaining these large-flowered foxgloves is to buy fresh seed each year from a reputable seed company. If you prefer the more elegant pale foxgloves, you can banish the purple forms with little effort by going over the seedlings that will appear around the original plants, and removing every one that has a flush of purple on the leaf stem. Those with plain green leaf stems will have pale flowers, though predicting whether white, primrose or peach is another matter.

Honesty, *Lunaria annua* (syn. *L. biennis*), is another biennial that obligingly seeds itself, and it also has two seasons of value: spring, when the lilac-purple flowers open, and fall, when the papery seedcases develop into "honesty money." Selections exist with white flowers (*alba*) or rich purple ('Munstead Purple') or with variegated leaves: 'Haslemere' has cream and green leaves and purple-lilac flowers,

LEFT *In the cool shadow of a copse, an informal serpentine wall, green with moss, retains a bank in which white sweet rocket,* Hesperis matronalis alba, *has seeded itself to gleam in the shadows. Ivy and the rampant* Lamium galeobdolon *keep the weeds at bay on the other side of the path, but will themselves need controlling.*

RIGHT *The biennial* Smyrnium perfoliatum *and white- or purple-flowered honesty,* Lunaria biennis *(syn. L. annua), both perpetuate themselves by self-seeding to make relaxed, minimum-care groups such as this in shaded corners.*

'Stella' white flowers over very white leaves. The variegations do not always show at first; give them time to develop before throwing out seedlings in the fear they will remain plain green. There is also a perennial honesty, *Lunaria rediviva*, with mauve flowers and more elliptical seedcases. The white honesty looks good with *Smyrnium perfoliatum*, a biennial with large, acid-yellow bracts in spring, resembling a spurge but actually related to cow parsley. Once established it should seed itself liberally from year to year.

The related sweet rocket, *Hesperis matronalis*, in lilac or white, is actually a perennial too but can be treated as a biennial, for it seeds itself freely and in summer fills the evening air with its warm, stock-like fragrance. It needs controlling in small gardens, but the effort is worth it for the perfume.

Spring is the season of forget-me-nots, often used as bedding among tulips, but just as at home in informal settings, drifting among shrubs or under orchard trees in thin grass. There are selections with deeper blue flowers, or with pink ones. If you are happy with the pale and pretty original forget-me-not, you can simply leave them to re-sow themselves each year. Pull them up as they begin to go over, or you will have more than you want.

Pale colors in the shadows

As night falls in the garden, it is the pale colors of flower and leaf that linger longest, seeming almost to hold their own moonlight within them. By bringing together a selection of plants with white-variegated, palely glaucous or silvered foliage, and white or very pale flowers–cream, primrose, ice-mauve, blush pink–you can create a subtle, moonlit planting in a shaded garden. It will be doubly effective against a dark background of clipped yew hedges or tall hollies, perhaps. Allow contrasts of darker foliage among the pale shades, too.

These groups will be most successful in part-day or dappled shade, or in the open-skied shadow of distant trees or buildings. Few plants flower freely in very dark places, as you will have deduced from the advice on page 18 about coping with problem shade. However tempting the idea of white flowers in dense, black shade, it really will not work.

BELOW **Left to right:** *Anemone narcissiflora, Fritillaria meleagris alba, Viola odorata* 'Alba' with *Convallaria majalis* (lily of the valley) behind, and *Tiarella cordifolia.* White foxgloves (*Digitalis purpurea alba*) give height behind, next to a common hazel (*Corylus avellana*). OPPOSITE ABOVE **Left to right:** *Primula denticulata, Astilbe* 'Praecox Alba,' *Astilboides tabularis, Hosta undulata undulata, Gentiana asclepiadea alba.*

A wildling group to tuck in among shrubs

Anemone narcissiflora: white flowers touched with mauve in heads of six or more on 2ft stems in early summer.
Convallaria majalis (lily-of-the-valley).

Digitalis purpurea alba (white foxglove): watch they do not smother small plants as they seed.
Fritillaria meleagris alba: exquisite albino of the snake's head fritillary.

Tiarella cordifolia: ivory, fluffy spikes over heart-shaped leaves in summer.
Viola odorata 'Alba': white sweet violets for early spring.

A group for moist soil

Astilbe 'Praecox Alba': small, dainty astilbe
with foamy white plumes in summer and
green, finely dissected foliage.
Astilboides tabularis (syn. *Rodgersia tabularis*):
large rounded leaves with shallow-scalloped
edges, of softest almond green.
Gentiana asclepiadea alba: white form of the
fall-flowering willow gentian.
Hosta undulata undulata: spiraling green leaves
with broad central white stripe.
Primula denticulata alba (white drumstick
primula): flowers in spring.

A border grouping

Hebe rakaiensis: low, wide evergreen dome of
apple-green foliage.
Nemophila maculata: white flowers with indigo
tips to the petals.
Philadelphus coronarius 'Bowles' Variety':
white-variegated leaves; fragrant cream
flowers in summer.
Phillyrea latifolia: glittering, dark evergreen
shrub.
Phlox 'Mia Ruys': short-growing and forms
quilts of white flowers in summer; warm,
peppery fragrance.

LEFT **Left to right:
front, *Hebe rakaiensis*,
Nemophila maculata,
Phlox 'Mia Ruys';
behind, *Phillyrea
latifolia*, *Philadelphus
coronarius* 'Bowles'
Variety.'**

CAMEOS AND COLLECTIBLES

If the plants in the previous chapter can be likened to the paintings on the walls of a room, those I want to suggest now are more like the small ornaments you might place on a mantelshelf. They are plants to look at closely, admiring their fine detail and line. Some of them are easy to grow, a few are more challenging. Some may captivate you so much that you want to collect the set, as it were; to track down all the celandines, or wood anemones, or the temperamental double primroses.

The wake robbins, species of Trillium, earn their botanical name from their structure—everything is in threes: three leaves, three calyces, and three petals. One of the most handsome and easygoing is T. grandiflorum, the wake robin, its white flowers here standing out against the dark foliage of Rheum australe (syn. R. emodi).

The small woodland wildlings

It is worth making a small bed of ideal garden soil (see page 26) for these and other little treasures. So long as it is in part or dappled shade, even an apparently hopeless corner of the garden can be transformed into a cameo. In one of my own gardens there was an awkward angle between the garage and a bank topped by an old apple tree. I shored up the base of the bank and filled in with barrow-loads of shade-garden soil, using the natural rather sandy loam of the bank as part of the mixture. Because I had plenty of thin slabs of sandstone, I made low stone walls to retain the bank (see page 92), but I could have used old railroad ties or logs instead.

Many of my precious woodlanders found an initial home in this angled bed, and I soon had enough of

several of them to transplant colonies among shrubs on the bank above, where they had to look after themselves. The price and commercial availability of a plant is a rough guide to its ease of cultivation: the more I have to pay, or the more trouble I have tracking it down, the more I am inclined to give a new shade plant a cosseted start in life. Thus you might be willing to risk the easier trilliums, relatives of the lilies with leaves and petals in threes, in less controlled surroundings; the wake robin, *Trillium grandiflorum* and several others are quite easy to obtain and are described in greater detail in the chapter on key plants (see page 118). The double wake robin, and some of the tiny species, are more elusive and deserve special treatment.

LEFT *The double wake robin,* Trillium grandiflorum flore-pleno, *is a shade-loving plant of rare beauty, deserving to stand alone, as it does here, in the best leafy soil that can be provided. If it is to be paired with anything, let its companions be the choicest blue poppies of pure tint such as* Meconopsis grandis *GS600 or* M. × sheldonii *'Slieve Donard.'*

Where winter aconites are happy they will thrive in the most unlikely conditions, on clay or sand. But they may refuse to grow in another garden. Try them first in ideal soil, and if they increase you can try them among your shrubs and under trees. *Eranthis hyemalis* 'Guinea Gold' is a superior form with large flowers on long stems, appearing with the common snowdrop, *Galanthus nivalis*.

Most Solomon's seals are easygoing, and their elegant, arching stems set with dangling alabaster bells look well among the more aristocratic shrubs. One of the choicest small species is *Polygonatum falcatum*, which slowly spreads into a thicket up to 1ft tall, less than half the height of the common *P. × hybridum* (syn. *P. multiflorum*). *P. falcatum* 'Variegatum' has leaves margined with pink-flushed white, and is charming with the pink lily-of-the-valley, *Convallaria majalis rosea*. Other Solomon's seals, plain or variegated, are described in the chapter on key plants (see page 116), together with the related merrybells, species of *Uvularia*. The related disporums enjoy a good leafy soil at first, too. *Disporum smithii* and *D. hookeri oreganum* have fresh green leaves masking their creamy bells in spring, followed by orange fruits; *D. sessile*, twice as tall at 2ft, has a cultivar 'Variegatum,' with narrow leaves striped with white. *D. flavens* has pendulous clusters of yellow flowers in spring.

The clintonias have leaves similar to lily-of-the-valley, but are slow spreaders unlikely to outlive their welcome in a leafy shade bed. *Clintonia andrewsiana* has clusters of rosy pink bells on 2ft stems followed by deep blue berries, and *C. borealis*, half as tall, has yellow-green flowers, while those of *C. umbellata* are white and scented. I have found *Reineckia carnea* more of a spreader though far from invasive, forming dense clumps of rather pale, grassy foliage decorated with starry pink flowers in early summer. The May lily, *Maianthemum bifolium*, is decidedly aggressive—one not for the special quarters, but for the shrub bed, where its lily-of-the-valley leaves can spread to form a harmless carpet topped by small creamy flowers in late spring.

The May apple of North America, *Podophyllum peltatum*, earns its name from its flowering season and its curious fruits, but it is the leaf that first catches the eye, as suggested by the common name of the other species you are likely to find available, the Asiatic *P. hexandrum* (syn. *P. emodi*), or umbrella leaf. Another umbrella leaf, *Diphylleia cymosa*, is much less common, and most striking when bearing its purple-blue fruits on reddish stems. Blue berries also distinguish *Caulophyllum thalictroides*, which has one large, divided leaf per stem, and deep blue fruits as big as marbles on 2ft stems. An exquisite rarity which may or may not be related to the podophyllums (botanists cannot agree) is *Glaucidium palmatum*, a Japanese woodlander with larger, fragile, poppy-like flowers in lavender or white, on 2ft stems over podophyllum-like leaves.

ABOVE *In a flowery copse in spring, hazels (*Corylus avellana*) make a friendly, leafy canopy for blue-flowered* Omphalodes cappadocica, *the evergreen spurge* Euphorbia amygdaloides var. robbiae, *white and pink bluebells, ferns, some pale yellow fritillaries and a solitary yellow Welsh poppy.*

Woodland flowers for spring and fall

The word "poppy" conjures up images of scarlet sun-lovers, but apart from the Himalayan blue poppies there are several poppy relatives which need cool, leafy soil and shelter from wind to thrive. The dawn poppy, *Eomecon chionanthum*, is likely to be too territorial for your special bed, but among shrubs it can run as much as it will. It has large, rounded leaves of glaucous tone, and nodding, white flowers with yellow stamens. The blood root, *Sanguinaria canadensis*, is better behaved, and as beautiful in pale, waxy leaf; in any case most people choose the double-flowered 'Plena,' for the pure white, full-petaled flowers last better than the fleeting single. Both these poppy relatives have red or orange sap, which bleeds if the roots are broken.

The celandine poppy, *Stylophorum diphyllum*, has pale green or bluish crimpled, hairy leaves and clear yellow poppies on 1ft stems in spring and summer; it seeds itself all too modestly, or can be divided. *Hylomecon japonicum*, which so far as I know has no common name, spreads slowly into a clump of fresh green, divided leaves over which lemon-yellow poppies float in spring. Of the Himalayan blue poppies and their yellow or white cousins, described in the chapter on key plants (see page 115), the only one I would admit in a bed of special treasures is *Meconopsis quintuplinervia*, the harebell poppy. The others merit the most careful attention to soil and shelter, but their scale demands that they be grown among shrubs (try *M. grandis* GS600 with *Azalea* 'Daviesii' and yellow primulas) or in the dappled shade of trees.

The harebell poppy has lavender-blue flowers, not the startling azure or ultramarine of its larger cousins. This tender coloring harmonizes with soft yellow, as for example the dwarf *Rhododendron* 'Shamrock.' Blue flowers invariably have a special appeal, and the Virginian bluebell of North American woodlands, *Mertensia pulmonarioides* (syn. *M. virginica*), is no exception. Its gray-green foliage is the ideal complement to the narrow, nodding bells, which open in spring on 1½ft stems. The whole plant dies down by midsummer.

Like the Virginian bluebell, most woodlanders flower in spring, but some wait until summer or even fall. *Deinanthe caerulea* is a plant of quiet charm, with nodding, fleshy, slate-blue flowers on reddish stems over rounded leaves. Far more striking, though it is all in shades of green, is *Daiswa polyphylla* (syn. *Paris polyphylla*), its whorls of pointed leaves topping the 3ft stems to support the intricate structure of radiating green sepals and thread-fine yellow-green petals that encircle the prominent purple stigma.

Most of the toad lilies, species of *Tricyrtis*, flower in late summer or fall. The taller kinds, yellow *T. latifolia*, freckled *T. formosana* and white, purple-blotched *T. hirta*, can look after themselves among shrubs, but I would give a special place to any of

but some that prefer cooler conditions, such as *F. pallidiflora* and *F. verticillata*, are described in the chapter on key plants (see page 109).

Even more bizarre than the toad lilies and fritillaries are the aroids. The mouse plant, *Arisarum proboscideum*, earns its name from the little maroon, long-tailed flowers that look like a whole family of mice seeking refuge among its carpet of little arrowhead leaves. Despite its diminutive size this is a willing spreader, better among shrubs than with slow-growing treasures. Another easy aroid is Jack-in-the-pulpit, *Arisaema triphyllum*, with green spathes often heavily striped with purple, followed by cylindrical spikes of gleaming scarlet berries.

Other arisaemas mimic snails (*A. griffithii*, its

those with shuttlecock flowers, such as *T. macrantha* var. *macranthopsis*. The starry white sprays of *Saxifraga cortusifolia fortunei* come in early fall, held in flights over broad, shining leaves with a maroon reverse. 'Wada' has this burgundy coloring on the upper surface of the leaf as well, making it a good companion for the claret-splashed toad lilies.

If frecklings and checkerings appeal to you, the fritillaries will be irresistible. The snake's head lily, *F. meleagris*, thrives in cool, damp soil in grass—in a few meadows in southern England that have been farmed by the same method for the last nine hundred years, huge colonies survive, coloring the grass with somber red-purple in late spring with here and there an alabaster-pale albino. Many fritillaries prefer sun,

curled spathe green to chocolate in color, with frilled edges netted with white veins), helmets (*A. ringens*), or serpents (*A. speciosum*, velvety maroon over a creamy spadix ending in a long, purple string). All these have dramatic foliage, three-lobed and shiny, the stems often mottled with brown on green. Others, such as *A. consanguineum*, have leaves divided into as many as 20 narrow leaflets. Two species are more beautiful than bizarre: *A. candidissimum*, with its pure white spathe striped with pale pink in the throat and green without, popping up suddenly at mid-summer from the bare soil and quickly followed by the broad leaves; and *A. sikokianum*, which has a trim, deep chocolate-maroon spathe clasping a broad ivory-white spadix in spring.

Wildlings domesticated

Dianella caerulea
Named after Diana, the goddess of the hunt, the dianellas are Southern-hemisphere lily relatives for warm, shady places. They are known as flax lilies in their native Australia, because of their tough, strong, evergreen leaves; this species is also called paroo lily. Its slender stems bear open sprays of small, starry, pale blue, yellow-anthered flowers, but its moment of glory comes in the fall when the gleaming, royal blue berries ripen, to last for several weeks.

In days gone by, gardening was very much a matter of utility; plants were grown for eating or for medicinal and household purposes more than for ornament. But people have always delighted in the curious, unusual or beautiful, so the primrose that sported a ruff of green around the petals (earning it the nickname Jack-in-the-green), or the wood anemone that forsook its blush-white tones for a tender blue, would be cherished. Sweet violets can be had in many manifestations, too, with the extra quality of fragrance, as their name *Viola odorata* tells us. They have the odd property of anaesthetizing the sense of smell, so that after the first delicious whiff you can inhale as much as you like without return. Leave them for a while; your olfactory organs will recover and be able to smell the violets again.

As well as the usual blue-violet and hardly less common white, sweet violets have been selected in rich violet-purple, azure blue and a blue as pale as skimmed milk, pink and rose, buff and amber. These tend to increase all too slowly, though the more common blue and white spread quite fast, and their running stems can be separated to make new colonies. Beware, in your shady bed of treasures, the pale slate-blue dog violets (*Viola canina* and *V. riviniana*), purple-leaved *V. labradorica* and pink *V. rupestris rosea*; they are invasively free-seeding, and the yellow *V. pensylvanica* and *V. glabella* are almost as bad. Keep them safely among shrubs, where they can do no harm, or with other lowly plants of equal vigor such as most of the small lamiums.

The butterfly-flowered scentless violets such as *Viola papilionacea* are better-behaved, and very beautiful with their large, wide-awake flowers. One of the finest is *V. obliqua alba*, its bold pure ·white flowers enlivened by fine pencilings of mauve on the lower petals. All this group die away to rhizomes to rest through the winter, so it is worth marking their place with a cane so as to avoid inadvertently planting something else in what looks like a nice empty patch of soil. The Pyrenean *V. cornuta* is more of a border plant, for it will weave its way through neighbors so that its perky lavender, white or near-blue flowers pop up in unexpected places. It holds its own, for example, with *Alchemilla mollis* and a muscular hosta such as *Hosta sieboldiana*, or will negotiate the low branches of a neighboring shrub.

The dog's tooth violet of European woods is not a true violet, but a diminutive lily relative. *Erythronium dens-canis* has smooth leaves mottled with maroon, and nodding flowers in shades of lilac-pink, purple or white. Some of the best have been given cultivar names and are worth growing in a bed of special shade soil (see page 108). Once you have plenty, try them in thinly grassed soil beneath trees. North America is the home of several beautiful erythronium species, often known as trout lilies on account of the marbling on their leaves. These, too, should spread quite freely if you give them the right leafy, cool soil, not too dry.

Wood anemones can increase rapidly, though their slender rhizomes and frail-stemmed leaves are unlikely to be a problem except among very tiny, precious plants. The blues and the doubles, and the creamy hybrid between *Anemone nemorosa* and the yellow *A. ranunculoides*, known as *A. × lipsiensis*, are especially enchanting at close quarters, yet all are quite well able to cope with rougher conditions and spread a carpet of flower in spring among the shrubs. Even quite small scraps of rhizome will grow, so when you lift a clump to plant it elsewhere, you are likely to finish up with what seems like almost as many in the original spot as in the new.

The ordinary celandine, *Ranunculus ficaria*, can be a pest in the garden, but its well-behaved cultivars merit special corners. Several are described in the chapter on key plants (see page 117); their flowers vary in color from pure white to coppery-orange, and in form from the simple single blooms to neatly formal doubles. One, originally found growing in a copse in southern England, has the usual shiny, bright lemon flowers, offset by almost black leaves, earning it the name 'Brazen Hussy.' Even more than the wood anemones, these special selections are worth starting in a pocket of leafy soil among stones before risking them among larger plants.

BELOW *Woodland wildlings—a pink form of the wood anemone,* Anemone nemorosa, *and wild violets,* Viola rupestris—*mingle in a spring group punctuated by the foliage of a geum, its tight buds poised to open later in spring. The violet can be invasive, with its free-seeding ways.*

ABOVE *Erythroniums such as these pink and white forms of* E. revolutum *are sometimes called trout lilies because of the marbling on their leaves. As the shape of their flowers suggests, they are related to the true lilies, but their roots are corms, not scaly bulbs. They are at their best in cool, leafy soil.*

89

ABOVE *One of the most exquisite of primroses is* Primula whitei, *which forms egg-like resting buds in winter, expanding in early spring to this rosette of white-mealed leaves encircling a cluster of ice-blue flowers with white eyes. Pamper it and other Petiolarid primulas with cool, leafy soil and a moist atmosphere.*

Primroses common and rare

Primroses are plants of cool shade, and the pale *Primula vulgaris* will seed itself on thinly grassed banks facing away from the sun, or under open-branched trees. Available in many different colors and aberrant structures–doubles, Jacks-in-the-green, and so on–they come and go, for they need regular division into fresh soil rich in organic matter and are apt to die out if they do not get it. They also very much dislike a dry atmosphere, so shelter from hot or desiccating winds is vital if they are to thrive. Primroses with the blood of *Primula juliae* are generally tougher than those of the pure *P. vulgaris* type; 'Wanda,' that popular bright magenta primrose, seems able to cope in almost any conditions. I have even seen it used as a kind of permanent bedding, alternating in formal clumps with *Viola labradorica purpurea* and *Lamium maculatum* 'Beacon Silver' in a symphony of purple, magenta and pink among contrasting purple and silver leaves.

Among the easier primroses of the *Primula vulgaris* type are var. *sibthorpii* in pale mauve, 'Groeneken's Glory' in brighter lilac-rose, and white 'Schnee-kissen.' The Garryarde primrose 'Guinevere' has dark leaves to set off its tender mauve-pink flowers; it crosses freely with the wild primrose, and some of the seedlings inherit the dark foliage, a charming combination when the flower color turns out to be cream or palest gray-white. The least distinct can simply be popped in any odd corner among shrubs, with any you particularly like kept under your eye. Blue primroses, though they cannot match a gentian for intensity and purity of tone, are a truer blue than many flowers called "blue" in catalogs. 'Blue Riband' is one of the easiest, only a little marred by its bright yellow eye.

Smaller than these full-sized primroses is 'Kinlough Beauty,' a pink, candy-striped polyanthus type, while there are others even daintier: 'Lady Greer' and 'McWatt's Cream' are perfect miniatures with cream flowers on slender stems. If you really relish a challenge, try some of the doubles. Peach-pink 'Sue Jervis' or the old double white 'Alba Plena' or double lilac 'Lilacina Plena,' also known as Quaker's bonnet, are among the easier doubles. New ones come and go, but a few of the old double and aberrant forms maintain a tenuous hold in cultivation. You can have a good deal of fun raising primroses from seed; some seed merchants offer selections likely to produce a good percentage of doubles, among which you might be lucky and raise a sky-blue reminiscent of 'Buxton's Blue' (probably now extinct), or a double jack such as the creamy white 'Dawn Ansell.'

The genus *Primula* is a very large and variable one, including species as easy as the drumstick primula, *P. denticulata*, with its rounded heads of lilac, white or purple flowers, and others that are a challenge to

the most expert gardener. Botanists divide the genus into groups such as Candelabra, which includes the moisture-loving *P. japonica* and others with flowers in whorls up the stem. In the Sikkimensis group are the giant cowslip *P. florindae* and the daintier *P. sikkimensis* itself, both cowslip-scented, as well as the miniature *P. ioessa*, not too tricky to grow, with white to violet scented hanging bells.

The Nivales and Petiolares groups are trickier; not surprisingly, perhaps, this is where some of the most beautiful species are to be found. *P. gracilipes* is one of the easiest Petiolarid primulas, with rosettes of pale green leaves around a posy of mauve-pink, yellow-eyed flowers. *P. edgeworthii* is more appealing, with mealy leaves and mauve, lemon-eyed

flowers; *P. whitei* and the exquisite *P. bhutanica* are even more beautiful, with ice-blue, white-eyed flowers amid mealy leaves. They retire to resting buds for the winter. *P. chionantha* is a Nivalid primula, with clusters of white, scented flowers held candelabra-fashion over narrow leaves.

Another primula that has shade gardeners full of admiration is *P. reidii williamsii*, one of the challenging but exquisite Soldanelloides primulas, with rosettes of hairy leaves and heads of nodding, wide bells, lavender-blue or (irresistibly) white, with a faint fragrance. *P. sieboldii* is more tolerant of heat and humidity than most primulas. Its flowers, appearing in spring, come in a variety of colors, including shades of pink, red, purple, lilac and white.

ABOVE *The wild primrose,* Primula vulgaris, *blooms early in the year, with* Cyclamen coum *in pink and white, white Lenten roses (*Helleborus orientalis*), and the pinkish flowers of* Pulmonaria officinalis. *Narcissi will follow, and the richly colored young shoots of peonies promise flowers in early summer as well.*

Raised beds for rarer plants

Plants such as rare primulas, the smaller trilliums and other small or uncommon woodlanders deserve a place where you can keep them under your eye and free from competition. One way to do this is to make a small raised bed, filled with the leafy, open mixture already described (see page 26) as ideal shade-garden soil. It has more than one advantage. Discreet plants that need to be met on intimate terms are brought closer to the eye, and to the nose if scent is one of their attributes; and, depending on the materials used to make the retaining walls, you can create crevices for plants that prefer to grow vertically as well as places for those of more conventional tastes.

Choose a site away from overhanging branches but shaded for more than half the day. The hotter and drier your climate, the more shade will be needed, especially from the midday and afternoon sun. Be prepared to water the bed in dry spells; being raised above the surrounding soil level it will tend to dry out faster. Make sure that the area is completely free of perennial weeds before you start building.

The material most suitable for this purpose is stone—ideally, slivers of sandstone. In the days before we became aware of the environmental risks of stripping peat bogs, special beds were often made of peat blocks, which had the advantage that plants with running roots such as the small vacciniums and gaultherias could knit the blocks together. But that could lead to all sorts of trouble if a traveling plant turned out to be just too intrepid, taking over the whole construction. Worse still, peat blocks easily became infested with creeping weeds, which also made their way inextricably into the roots of the small peat-loving treasures.

Stone, on the other hand, is permanent, runs no risk of drying and shrinking in periods of drought, and provides a cool refuge for the roots of your special plants. You can also use old railroad ties or tree trunks, but in that case would need to use trailing plants such as *Persicaria vaccinifolia* (syn. *Polygonum vaccinifolium*), *Campanula poscharskyana* or *Asarina procumbens* to soften the edges and side walls of the bed. For acid soils there is gentian-blue *Lithodora diffusa* (syn. *Lithospermum diffusum*). These are vigorous plants, as they need to be to make an impression on a wall of two or three railroad ties' height. With a planting of small treasures that might be swamped by these energetic spreaders, choose instead clump-forming plants loose enough in growth to swell over the edge: mossy saxifrages, *Geranium dalmaticum*, the dwarf albino ivy-leaved toadflax (*Cymbalaria muralis* 'Nana Alba') and the like.

Building a stone wall

Before you begin, make sure you have a good supply of suitable stone–slivers of sandstone are ideal. You will also need ample quantities of fluffy, leafy soil, mixed beforehand. Sort the stones roughly by size, choosing the larger ones for the base of the wall. When building retaining walls for an existing bed or bank, you will need to improve the soil behind as there will be limited scope for adding new soil.

● *Sink the lower half of each stone in the bottom layer into the soil and tilt it slightly upwards. This gives extra stability as well as helping to ensure that rain will run between the stones and into the soil rather than washing the soil out.*

● *As each layer is added, sift some of your soil between the stones as though it were mortar, and pack it firmly behind the stones as you go. Remember to lay the stones so that the vertical spaces are not all one above the other.*

RIGHT *Equally at home on the flat, in the rock garden or growing vertically, tucked into the crevices of a wall, as here, with its roots reaching into cool soil,* Geranium dalmaticum *is a good-tempered little plant, bearing its lilac-pink flowers over rounded, glossy foliage. It combines prettily with small ferns such as the black spleenwort (*Asplenium adiantum-nigrum*), which also appreciates cool conditions.*

PLANTS TO GROW VERTICALLY IN RAISED-BED WALLS

Asplenium ruta-muraria (wall rue): a fern with little sprays of rue-like fronds.

Boykinia jamesii: cherry-pink flowers in early summer; best in lime-free soil, not too rich.

Ceterach officinarum (ric-rac fern): tiny fronds resembling needleworker's trimming.

Corydalis ochroleuca: gray-green divided leaves and ivory-white fumitory flowers; keep away from smaller plants.

Cymbalaria muralis 'Nana Alba': miniature white ivy-leaved toadflax.

Geranium dalmaticum: miniature geranium with shiny leaves and pink or white flowers in summer.

Haberlea and *Ramonda* species, described in the chapter on key plants, (see pages 112 and 117): flat rosettes of crinkled leaves.

● *Once you have built up a layer or two, the real fun starts as you tuck in plants between the stones as you go.*

A raised bed in shade

Rarer and more delicate plants can be pampered in a raised bed: for example, you can mix your soil to suit either lime-tolerant or acid-loving plants which might not thrive elsewhere in your garden.

As well as the acid-lovers shown below, you could grow the rare poppy relative *Pteridophyllum racemosum* with its white flowers and ferny leaves, *Polygala chamaebuxus grandiflora*, a milkwort with keeled, yellow and magenta flowers, and ourisias —creeping plants with white, scarlet or pink flowers in early summer. In ordinary soil the summer gentians such as *Gentiana septemfida* will thrive, as will other treasures such as *Aquilegia viridiflora* with its fragrant green and maroon flowers.

BELOW **Left to right:** *Epigaea gaultherioides, Corydalis cashmeriana, Gentiana sino-ornata, Andromeda polifolia* 'Nikko,' *Shortia soldanelloides*.

Shade plants for a raised bed filled with acid soil

Andromeda polifolia 'Nikko': little mounds of blue-gray foliage and large rose-pink urn-shaped flowers.
Corydalis cashmeriana: dissected, gray-green leaves and clusters of sky-blue flowers.

Epigaea gaultherioides (syn. *Orphanidesia gaultherioides*): leathery leaves on prostrate stems; flowers are open cups of soft pink.
Gentiana sino-ornata: Chinese gentian with large, ultramarine flowers in the fall.

Shortia soldanelloides: rounded, toothed leaves, burnished in winter; open, fringed bells, pink fading to white at the margins, in spring. Where they thrive, the shortia and epigaea make effective small-scale ground-cover.

Lime-tolerant shade plants for a raised bed

Dicentra cucullaria: finely divided leaves and white, lemon-tipped flowers in early summer.
Dodecatheon pulchellum 'Red Wings': crimson, cyclamen-like flowers over smooth basal foliage.

Iris cristata: tiny crested iris with lavender-blue, orange-crested flowers.
Jeffersonia dubia: single, cupped, lilac-blue flowers in spring, followed by kidney-shaped leaves with scalloped margins.

Soldanella villosa: velvety-furred leaves, and violet, fringed flowers in spring.
Ramonda myconi: grows even better vertically than on the flat; rosettes of crinkled, dark leaves and lavender or white flowers.

Capturing fragrance

Cestrum parqui
Releasing its sweet, far-carrying fragrance only at night, during the day this plant is scentless. If bruised it retaliates with the sour smell typical of the potato family, to which it belongs. Shrubby in mild climates, it behaves like a herbaceous plant in colder areas, flowering later but with larger heads than on unpruned plants.

Intimacy in the garden is not simply a question of size. It also has to do with design, and especially with atmosphere. Humans are very visual animals, so we tend to think first of shape and color in the garden; but there are other elements to the ambiance that we create, and fragrance is one of the most powerful. It has the capacity to stir the emotions and to evoke memories we thought lost for ever.

It is for its poignant fragrance, above all, that I value the eye-catching *Daphne odora*; it is with their honeyed perfume, floating on the cold air, that the sarcococcas win our hearts; and everyone forgives the lily-of-the-valley its walkabout ways when, in late spring, the deliciously scented white bells open and we can gather posies for the house.

Shady gardens are often sheltered gardens, and that makes them especially suited for those who love fragrance, for wind is the enemy of scent, blowing it away; but in a sheltered place fragrance is captured, lingering on the air. If you have an exposed garden, one of the ways you can create instant shelter and shade, as well as a pleasant place to sit, is by building the garden construction known as a lath house.

This consists of a framework to which you fix laths, spaced so you have equal proportions of lath and gap. The laths should run north to south on the roof, and vertically on the walls, to ensure the maximum movement in the pattern of sun and shade during the day. If you intend to use your lath house for sitting as well as growing, it is worth having a back-up frame or two covered with lath panels, so that you can move container-grown plants to and fro –into the lath house when at their best, back into the frame when looking less than perfect.

You can also make raised beds, or plant directly in the soil within the house; but this is unsafe if there are trees nearby, for their roots will quickly invade the lath house beds to steal the rich mixture provided for your special plants.

Even in temperate southern England, to say nothing of hotter or windier climates, a lath house can be invaluable for tricky plants such as shortias, certain primulas, plants with leaves that easily burn in sun or wind such as *Begonia grandis evansiana*, or even for choice ferns and tender rhododendrons that will spend the winters in frost-free quarters.

Outside the lath house, in borders and shrub plantings, there is fragrance in plenty to be had from many of the plants already mentioned in these pages: the yellow day lilies, *Hemerocallis*, *Lilium pyrenaicum*, the mock oranges, *Philadelphus*, and the Mexican orange, *Choisya ternata*, the giant cowslip, *Primula*

Using a lath house

In temperate climates a lath house can provide invaluable protection for delicate or difficult plants, and in hotter regions it can shelter lush greenery. A simple construction, it creates the ideal environment for the garden-owner to relax in, surrounded by the captured fragrance of scented rhododendrons, Oriental lilies and tobacco flowers.

florindae, sweet rocket, sweet violets, phlox, and the great tobacco *Nicotiana sylvestris* among them.

At the very turn of the year there is the delicate perfume of snowdrops: the best way to enjoy their honey scent is to pick a little bunch for the house. Fragrant posies are especially welcome in winter, and to the snowdrops we can add sprigs of witch hazel for their spicy perfume, or a spray or two of *Azara microphylla* for its vanilla-custard aroma, honeyed sarcococca, *Mahonia japonica* with its lily-of-the-valley scent, and perhaps even a precocious primrose.

Roses, wisteria and jasmine, the classic scented climbers, are plants for sunny places. The honey-suckles, which grow as well in shade as in sun, are not all fragrant, though as we shall see on page 98, those that are can fill the air with their perfume, especially at dusk. *Clematis montana*, above all among climbers, is the shade-gardener's friend, for its ability to grow where almost nothing else will, for its white flowers gleaming in the shadows and, as an extra bonus, for its vanilla scent. Pink-flowered montanas lose much of their color in the shade, and in any case the deepest in tone generally have the least fragrance, or none at all.

In spring, while we admire the little plants of the woodland floor, we may be bathed in fragrance from the white chalices of *Magnolia salicifolia* overhead; as spring advances into summer, the lime-tolerant *M. wilsonii* or acid-loving *M. sieboldii* take over, their white, crimson-eyed saucers dispensing scent in their turn. In gardens planted by someone exceptionally gifted with foresight or patience, it might be *M. × wieseneri*, a sprawling shrubby tree with rich creamy flowers endowed with perfume enough to fill an average garden and spill over into the neighbors'.

You need a very sheltered corner, or frost-free winter cover, to succeed with the lily-flowered rhododendrons such as 'Fragrantissimum,' 'Lady Alice Fitzwilliam,' or the wholly lovely *R. veitchianum*, which is at its best in the Cubitii group. Many much hardier rhododendrons are scented, too, though few can compete with the swooning lily perfume of 'Fragrantissimum' and its kin. Nearest in

style to these is *R. johnstoneanum* in white or creamy primrose. The big, tree-like Loderi rhododendrons are fragrant, and so is the more compact *R. decorum*, while several azaleas, most notably the Piedmont azalea, *R. canascens*, have a terrific perfume. Some rhododendrons have aromatic foliage; *R. oreotrephes*, with its subtle color scheme of bluish foliage and lilac-mauve bells, and the little *R. glaucophyllum*, a favorite for small gardens, with white-backed leaves and old-rose bells, both smell deliciously of stables, for instance.

ABOVE *One of the attributes of* Clematis montana *is its vanilla fragrance. Gloomy corners hold no terrors for this easygoing climber, which will grow equally well on a dark, shady wall or, as here, through the branches of a host tree. Its pure white flowers reflect all the available light.*

Evoking perfumed nights

For people who can only enjoy their gardens after work or in the busy weekend hours–probably the majority of us–plants that are most fragrant at night have a special value, above all if they bear pale flowers that gleam in the shadows. They help to create a sense of peace and tranquility, a refuge from the day's stress. Even if it is not warm enough to sit out–as it may not be in spring when *Daphne odora* is flowering–a stroll around the garden can revive tired senses and soothe frayed nerves. By the time summer comes it is good to be able to spend the evening hours in the garden, eating alfresco perhaps, or reading, or simply sitting.

Some plants are more generous with their perfume at night: in shady places these include honeysuckles such as *Lonicera periclymenum*, the woodbine, and the cultivars 'Belgica' and 'Serotina,' which between them fill several summer months with flower and scent. Before these begin, the perfoliate honeysuckle, *L. caprifolium*, opens its creamy flowers, while the evergreen *L. japonica*, which starts to flower in early summer, may still be bearing blooms at the first frosts. Honeysuckles can be grown on a rough hedge, into a tree (avoiding anything too precious, for their twining stems can strangle a host), or on a specially erected trellis, arch or arbor.

If you used all these plants together, and even allowing for the fact that not all of them flower at the same time, you would create more of an assault on the olfactory nerves than an evocation of perfumed nights. The cestrum and hemerocallis could form part of a border grouping in shades of yellow and

LEFT *Embowering a lichen-covered stone seat, the woodbine or honeysuckle,* Lonicera periclymenum *'Serotina,' pushes a fragrant cluster of pink and cream flowers into the embrace of* Actinidia kolomikta, *of which the white-and-pink-variegated leaves glow in the shadows.*

RIGHT *The stately spires of* Nicotiana sylvestris, *their white trumpets perfumed all day as well as at night, are silhouetted against the shadowed side of a clipped beech hedge in this enclosed garden of fragrance. The much smaller* N. langsdorfii *at its feet is unscented but merits close inspection.*

green, incorporated perhaps into the partnerships suggested in the chapter on the decor (see pages 66–7). Seed of night-scented stocks can be scattered in many an odd corner, among shrubs perhaps; an ideal place is beneath a window that you open frequently in summer, so that their exquisite perfume can float in to sweeten the whole room. Oriental lilies can be grown in pots, to be stood on a patio or indoors while in flower, though some people find their fragrance too overwhelming indoors.

Sweet rocket and evening primrose are both plants that seed themselves around, so they can be encouraged to spread through informal borders or shrub plantings; their pale colors gleam in the dusk, tempting you over to admire them and, in so doing, to surrender yourself to their scent.

The tobacco flower and mignonette are not showy annuals, but their fragrance earns them a place among the plants you choose for sitting areas, on the cool side of a patio perhaps, or tucked around the seat in a secluded bower—which could be formed by honeysuckle trained over an arch or framework.

Both the Daphne and the Marvel of Peru (*Mirabilis jalapa*) make rounded, low bushes, though the Daphne is visually the better plant year-round. I like to plant the Daphne by a door that is often used, so that in its brief season you do not miss the elusive but poignant fragrance. The Marvel of Peru flowers for long months in summer, and in bright climates does very well in positions where it seldom or never receives direct sun. It needs to be overwintered in frost-free conditions.

PLANTS FOR EVENING FRAGRANCE

Cestrum parqui: for light shade only; tall spires of yellow-green flowers.

Daphne odora: creamy-white flowers.

Hemerocallis citrina: citron-yellow flowers opening in the evening.

Hesperis matronalis: white or pale lilac flowers; far-carrying clove perfume.

Lilium orientale: richly perfumed, wide, white flowers, often heavily blotched with crimson.

Lonicera periclymenum 'Graham Thomas': profuse, creamy fragrant flowers in summer and early fall.

Matthiola bicornis: night-scented stock.

Mirabilis jalapa: white, pink, crimson or yellow flowers open in early evening; free-floating fragrance.

Nicotiana alata grandiflora: khaki-backed white petals unfold at night to release a powerful fragrance.

Reseda odorata (mignonette): happy in part-shade.

THROUGH
THE SEASONS

Each of the seasons has its own character and its own tasks, so that the gardener is sometimes observer, sometimes participant. As you breathe the perfume-laden air about a honeysuckle or a drift of lilies, your reverie may be broken by the sight of a weed; intent on pruning a sapling, you may be seized by the beauty of the light shining through the leaves.

Fall foliage looks its best against a dark background of conifers or other evergreens such as this weeping cedar (Cedrus libani *var.* atlantica *'Glauca Pendula'*). If you can also contrive to see them against the sun shining through the fall leaves, as with this maple (Acer japonicum) *and fothergilla, they will seem almost incandescent in the days before they fall.*

Winter

Gardens that rely on color above all often look derelict in winter, but a garden that has been built within a sound framework of trees and evergreen foliage will be as effective at midwinter as at any other season. If your climate is so severe that evergreens have to be burlapped in the fall before vanishing beneath a mantle of snow, then only the silhouettes of trees will remain to be seen; but even these can be graceful or bold. A stand of birch against a snow-laden sky, with its haze of madder-purple twigs above white stems, has a quiet drama to it; while below, spring woodlanders lie protected beneath a blanket of snow, waiting for the thaw. In less extreme climates, a single deciduous magnolia that has been carefully pruned to reveal its clean, spare lines can be as beautiful when bare of leaf as it is when in bloom, later in the year.

In still milder, but by no means frost-free, climates, the earliest camellias such as *C. × williamsii* 'November Pink' will be flowering on sunless walls, and the crimson buds of *Skimmia japonica* 'Rubella' will foreshadow the fragrance of the flowers as they open in spring. Now is the time for *Helleborus atrorubens* to open its nodding, muted-red blooms, and for snowdrops (*Galanthus × atkinsii* is one of the earliest), winter aconites (*Eranthis hyemalis*) and *Cyclamen coum* to jewel the ground beneath trees and shrubs, along with the marbled, spear-head leaves of *Arum italicum marmoratum*. Female skimmias and aucubas bear gaudy scarlet berries and yellow *Jasminum nudiflorum* is in bloom.

Witch hazels (*Hamamelis*) are starred with their spicy-scented flowers in winter; the pale spidery petals of *H. × intermedia* 'Pallida' or 'Moonlight' are set off by the near-black leaves of *Ophiopogon planiscapus nigrescens*, and the tawny reds matched by cold-crimsoned *Tellima grandiflora* or bergenias.

Snow on Cyclamen *leaves, with snowdrops* (Galanthus nivalis) *and the papery seedheads of honesty (*Lunaria annua*).*

Evergreen ground-cover provided by *Liriope muscari*, *Gaultheria procumbens*, *Epimedium perralderianum* and pachysandra lends unity and solidity to the garden in winter. It also helps to insulate the soil against heat loss, and to prevent leafy mulches from blowing about the garden or being scattered on paths by birds.

Winter tasks

Cosmetic

● Cut away old leaves of Lenten roses so that in spring the flowers will hold the stage.
● Cut away frosted fern fronds, especially where winter or early spring bulbs are growing between the fern clumps.
● Pick fallen leaves and twigs off moss, ferns and small plants. Add the leaves directly to the mulch beneath shrubs and around taller plants, ensuring that they do not pile up around the collar (see "Fall"), or stack them to rot into leaf mold.

Routine maintenance

● Check newly planted trees, shrubs and perennials after frosty spells, and if the roots have been lifted, firm them back in with fists or the heel of your boot.
● Also check all small plants, many of which have shallow roots easily lifted out of fluffy shade-garden soil by frost; tuck them back in firmly after each frosty spell.
● Make sure that mulches are not building up too thickly around the collar of trees and shrubs, in case collar rot should set in.
● Prune clematis that flower after midsummer on new growth, such as the *Clematis viticella* hybrids; cut back to a pair of stout buds close to the ground (in areas with severe winters wait until late winter/early spring).
● If the job was not done in summer as the flowers fade, cut out last season's flowered shoots of Philadelphus.

More serious winter work

● Plant hardy, deciduous shrubs and trees.
● Remove the lower branches of trees that need limbing up (if you did not have time to do the job at mid-summer).
● Thin out thicket-forming shrubs by cutting old branches right out at the base.

Protecting plants

● Frost-protection of susceptible plants should have been set up in the fall, but be prepared to take emergency action by draping plants likely to suffer from severe weather with frost fabric, wind/frost protector of woven plastic, or even sheets of newspaper laid over small plants at night.
● If heavy snowfalls threaten to damage the woody framework of trees and shrubs, knock the snow off to reduce the weight. Low-growing plants and those not at risk of physical damage should be left under their blanket of snow as it is an effective insulator.

Spring

In sheltered places, primroses, violets and the first pulmonarias will be showing flowers in early spring, and the wood anemones will be starting to shoulder through the mossy soil beneath the still leafless trees. Between shrubs, Lenten roses and bergenias are flowering: plum-colored Lenten roses make a somber contrast beneath pale corylopsis, while white and green forms make cool pictures with *Ribes laurifolium* and *Skimmia × confusa* 'Kew Green.' Camellias and the earliest rhododendrons add a more exotic note, and the rosy buds of *Skimmia japonica* have begun to burst to release their lily-of-the-valley perfume.

Many of the plants of the woodland floor flower in spring, before the canopy above excludes much of the sun's light: epimediums and toothworts, dog's tooth violets and trilliums, Solomon's seal, Virginian bluebell and lily-of-the-valley. As the camellia season comes to an end in later spring, rhododendrons are in full bloom and the vivid spring foliage of *Pieris* frames sprays of white bells. The young growths of rhododendrons grown for their foliage can be as beautiful as flowers; *Rhododendron macabeanum*, for example, has scarlet bud scales yielding to silvered young leaves.

The new shoots of herbaceous plants—peonies in crimson and dove-pink young leaf, the bright swords of day lilies, and the shell-case snouts of hostas—promise flowers and foliage to come. Some border plants are in flower in late spring. Bleeding hearts (*Dicentra spectabilis*), *Geranium macrorrhizum* with its strongly aromatic leaves, and the blue forget-me-not-flowered *Brunnera macrophylla* or lowly *Omphalodes cappadocica* would make a soft harmony of pink and blue, joined by the pink cow parsley, *Chaerophyllum hirsutum* 'Roseum,' and *Geranium maculatum*. The cheerful yellow daisies of doronicums and sharp green of spurges and

Primroses and Fritillaria meleagris *both do well in moist soil, leafy or thin-grassed, beneath trees or among shrubs.*

the spurge-like *Smyrnium perfoliatum* echo the unfurling young shoots of oaks.

The poignant fragrance of *Daphne odora* fills the cold evening air, and overhead *Clematis montana* flings its white or rosy wreaths, while the first of the honeysuckles, *Lonicera caprifolium*, hints at summer to come with its sweet, free-floating perfume.

Spring tasks

Planting
- Plant hardy trees and shrubs, perennials and bulbs supplied in active growth, such as snowdrops.
- Beware of desiccating, cold winds, which can do more damage than drought to the emerging foliage of shade plants: be prepared to put up temporary screens until permanent shelter has grown.
- In warm, sunny spells, spraying the foliage of newly planted or susceptible plants can

help to reduce transpiration. Most vulnerable are new, unfurling leaves and those which are thin-textured and easily burnt.
- Later in spring, plant evergreen trees and shrubs that are not fully hardy in your area.

Propagation
- Increase hostas: cut wedges out of established clumps as if cutting a cake.
- Sow seed of half-hardy annuals.

Maintenance
- Remove the dead tops from herbaceous plants that were not tidied up in the fall.
- Apply a general-purpose fertilizer around plants growing in poor soil, for example under greedy trees (if using dry granules, wash any fertilizer dust off leaves; liquid fertilizer is less likely to burn plants).
- Top up mulches to keep plant roots cool during the hot days of summer.
- Clip ivy grown on a wall.
- Weed out foxglove seedlings with purple stains on the leaf stalk if you want to retain pure selections of white, apricot or primrose.
- Cut out winter-damaged shoots and dead or diseased wood from shrubs and trees.
- In early spring, prune *Hydrangea paniculata* and remove the flowerheads of mophead hydrangeas. This is also a good time to cut out the oldest stems of *H. macrophylla*.
- If winter-flowering mahonias have grown leggy, cut the stems hard back.
- Cut away the old fronds of hart's tongue and shield ferns.
- Watch for sudden late frosts, and be prepared to cover vulnerable plants at night.
- As early-flowering rhododendrons and azaleas fade, dead-head them.
- Dead-head camellias.
- Keep an eye out for slugs. Apply slug bait around susceptible subjects such as primulas and hostas. ·

Summer

Trees and shrubs are now in full leaf, and most of the woodland flowers are over, their brief cycle ended. But the shady garden still has much to offer, in both flower and leaf. The bold leaves of hostas and veratrum contrast with the finely dissected foliage of astilbes, cimicifugas and ferns. In shaded borders and among shrubs, day lilies and hardy geraniums begin their flowering season; the later deciduous azaleas are in flower, and the wide-spreading branches of lacecap viburnums are covered with a froth of white flowers.

As summer ripens, the warm air is full of the fragrance of tobacco flowers, honeysuckle and phlox; pale flowers gleam from the shadows in the long summer evenings. This is the time of year when gardeners appreciate shade even more than do their plants; a time to relax beneath the friendly branches of a tree, or to retreat with a good book into the lath house.

In early summer the climbing *Hydrangea petiolaris* bears its white lacecap flowers, followed in high summer by the related, and more declamatory, *Schizophragma integrifolium*. Late summer brings the big shrubby *Hydrangea aspera villosa* and velvet-leaved *H. sargentiana*.

Summer tasks

Cosmetic

● Remove weeds from shade beds and compost them. Hand-weeding is quick and easy in ideal shade soil, and enables you to leave desirable self-sown seedlings such as *Mertensia virginica*, *Cyclamen hederifolium*, *Stylophorum diphyllum*, and others that can be left to grow on where they are, potted, or moved to other parts of the garden.
● Hand-weed mossy patches that you want to encourage, carefully removing all weed seedlings, including grass.

Hemerocallis *'Pink Damask' and the blue-gray leaves of* Macleaya microcarpa *in a shaded summer border.*

● Dead-head plants running to seed, unless you want to save seed or allow them to naturalize (setting seed gives them less energy to produce fine foliage or next year's flowers).
● Cut plants such as *Alchemilla mollis*, *Tellima grandiflora*, *Hemerocallis lilioasphodelus* and pulmonarias to the ground and water well–new leaves will soon grow to remain comely for the rest of the season.
● If you have snake's head fritillaries growing in thin grass, do not cut the grass until after mid-summer, to allow the seed to ripen.
● If you have access to green bracken fern, cut the fronds as soon as they are fully expanded at mid-summer, and chop them to use as a mulch around small plants in the shade garden, or around any plant that is not thriving: green bracken fern is rich in nutrients and is an excellent tonic for plants.
● Cut out flowered stems of *Symphytum × uplandicum* 'Variegatum' to encourage the boldest variegations on new leaves.

● Shear back *Viola cornuta* as the flowers fade. They should then be watered and fed to encourage new growth and a second flush of flowers later in the season.
● Stake bulbs, such as lilies, and perennials that are growing in low light levels.
● Continue dead-heading rhododendrons and azaleas as the flowers fade.
● Soon after mid-summer, feed camellias to encourage buds for next year's blooms.
● As summer advances, dead-head border phloxes, cutting back to the first pair of leaves below the flower clusters.

Major tasks

● Open out cluttered trees (see page 20).

Watering

● If irrigation is needed, it is better to give ample quantities now and then rather than a sprinkling at shorter intervals.

Planting and propagation

● Plant pot-grown corms of *Cyclamen hederifolium*: they establish far more readily than those sold "dry."
● Plant out *Nicotiana sylvestris* to follow on from foxgloves.
● In late summer, collect fern spores from your own or friends' ferns (see page 56).
● Sow seed of hellebores as soon as they ripen. Lenten roses are unlikely to come true, but you may get some interesting seedlings.
● Collect berries from *Daphne mezereum*, rub off the flesh and sow the seeds immediately. In some areas birds take these berries almost before they are ripe; to beat the birds, collect the berries as soon as they start to show color.
● Sow seeds of peonies as soon as they ripen. The fertile seeds of *Paeonia mlokosewitchii* and others like it are black or dark blue; do not waste your time sowing infertile scarlet or crimson seeds.

Fall

A second spring comes to the shady garden, as willow gentian, toad lilies, cimicifugas and *Kirengeshoma palmata* flower with the scented *Hosta* 'Royal Standard,' and the marbled leaves of *Arum italicum marmoratum* develop as the scarlet berries fall. *Liriope muscari* bears its bright mauve spikes to contrast with pink or white colchicums, and *Cyclamen hederifolium* is covered with flights of pink or white flowers. The white stars of *Saxifraga fortunei* contrast with lilac-blue *Crocus speciosus* and *C. goulimyi.*

Overhead, *Pileostegia viburnoides* bears its cones of creamy froth, making a fine backdrop for pink Japanese anemones, late hostas such as violet-spiked *H. lancifolia*, and the foliage of *Symphytum × uplandicum* 'Variegatum.' More typical of fall are the bright berries of *Actaea* and the orange seeds of *Iris foetidissima.* Hosta foliage turns to gold, the rounded leaves of *Galax urceolata* begin to burnish, and the foliage of *Mahonia aquifolium* takes on its rich winter colors. The first of the winter-flowering mahonias, *M. × media* 'Lionel Fortescue,' shows its yellow candles.

Shade-giving trees such as mountain ashes and *Crataegus persimilis* 'Prunifolia' are in fruit, with shrubs like the Guelder rose, *Viburnum opulus*, in red or yellow translucent berry. The flowers of mophead hydrangeas take on metallic tones of verdigris, copper and burnished red.

Fall tasks

● Except where winters are severe, or the soil is heavy and lies wet in winter, plant hardy deciduous shrubs and trees. Make sure the planting hole is large enough to take the roots spread outwards, to give the plant a secure hold against wind-rock and frost-lifting.

● In areas with mild winters, hardy evergreens can be planted in early fall.

The dying leaves of the Japanese maple, Acer japonicum *'Aconitifolium,' flare into scarlet and vermilion in the fall.*

● Plant hardy, spring-flowering perennials, spring bulbs, hardy biennials such as foxgloves and honesty, and "pips" (sections of root with a growth bud) of lily-of-the-valley.

● Unwrap mail-order plants, and soak the roots to help them recover from drying during transit.

● If mail-order plants arrive during a frosty spell, wrap them again in wet burlap and store them in a cool but not frosty place until conditions improve.

● Where you have been able to maintain a thick mulch of leaves, the soil beneath may remain workable even in frosty spells. Plants could be heeled in among shrubs after drawing the mulch aside. If the soil is wet after a spell of heavy rain but you cannot wait to plant, fill among the roots with good shade soil (see page 26) which has been kept under cover so it is on the dry side. Do not use dry peat, as the roots may become dry through contact with the peat.

Divide shade plants

● To increase established clumps of lily-of-the-valley, dig out square clods of soil and root and set them elsewhere in the garden, with minimum disturbance.

● In early fall divide hardy spring-flowering perennials and ferns.

Routine maintenance

● Clear fallen leaves from small plants.

● Rake leaves from grass paths and lawn.

● Add these leaves to the natural leaf fall among shrubs. Except around small plants the mulch can be as much as 5in deep; apply the leaves wet in tight handfuls, keeping them away from the stems of woody plants to avoid the risk of collar rot.

● If you have access to bracken fern rhizomes, smash them flat with the back of a spade and add them to the leafy mulch.

● Use other organic materials (see page 26) to mulch and nourish shade plants.

Prepare for winter

● Plants that will be damaged if the soil freezes around their roots need a thick mulch to help them safely through winter.

● In climates with very cold winters, wrap evergreen shrubs in burlap.

● Protect plants of borderline hardiness in milder winter areas with burlap screens (to keep off cold winds and frost), heaped coarse bark, leaves or bracken fern around plants that are able to regenerate from the base, and plastic overcoats to keep off excess moisture (allow air to circulate around the plant, sealing it in its plastic wrap at times of extreme cold, when an inner lining of straw or dry bracken fern will also help to protect it).

● Wrap the pot of container-grown plants in bubble plastic, or heap sawdust, bark or fallen leaves over them to a depth of 1ft to keep out frost.

KEY PLANTS FOR SHADY GARDENS

The plants in this chapter are a personal selection of those which I, as a dedicated shade gardener, would not want to be without. Of course, it is unlikely that any garden except a very large one would be able to accommodate them all. They are described here to help you make a selection, with due regard to your soil and climate, the size of your garden, and your own taste.

The flowers of Viburnum plicatum 'Mariesii' are so abundant in their early summer season, and the leaves so fresh and green, that the shrub looks as though a white, lacy shawl draped on green velvet has been flung over the tiered branches. In the fall the flowers give way to red fruits amid the crimson and wine-purple dying leaves. V. plicatum 'Shasta' is similar but flowers a little later, and remains more compact in maturity.

Simply choosing plants is only the first step. The way to transform a collection of plants into a garden, with all that the word implies in terms of aesthetic experience and emotional repose, is to create a design that suits the site and the owner's needs, and to set the plants within it in juxtapositions and partnerships that bring out their own best qualities. That is why each entry concludes with a couple of suggested planting partners.

In some cases these suggestions are very specific; take the entry, *Actaea* (baneberry), as an example. The suggested partners are *Gentiana asclepiadea* and *Tricyrtis hirta*—that is, not just the genus, but also the species is indicated. Even within that apparent precision, however, there is scope for your own inventiveness. If you like the elegance of white and green, you will choose *Actaea alba*, *Gentiana asclepiadea alba*, and *Tricyrtis hirta alba*. Change the baneberry to *Actaea spicata*, and you have a black-and-white scheme. Change again to *Actaea erythrocarpa*, ordinary *Tricyrtis hirta* and *Gentiana asclepiadea* 'Phyllis' and you have a subtle scheme of maroon, dusky lilac and pale blue. If you read the entries for these plants in the pages that follow, you will see that that is far from the end of the possible partnerships you could devise with those three alone, quite apart from others that seem good to you.

Lastly, a note on hardiness: this is a relative matter, for a plant that is hardy with you may not be with me, and vice versa. It is partly (but not wholly) to do with temperature. The plant hardiness map (see page 124) and the zones indicated in the index (see pages 124–128) provide further guidance on the plants that can be grown most successfully in your garden.

Bulbs, corms and tubers

Cyclamen

The fall-flowering *C. hederifolium* and late winter-flowering *C. coum* in its many variants are hardy and easy woodlanders, increasing–often quite rapidly–by seed in leafy soil. The first has leaves showing a wide range of marblings and markings from almost plain green to heavily silvered. *C. coum* has more rounded leaves, also varying in their markings, and stubbier flowers, almost always with a pink "nose." For more sheltered places *C. repandum* has elegant deep pink flowers in early summer, and *C. purpurascens* bears its scented flowers in late summer over marbled leaves.

Size H: 4in; S: 4in–1ft. **Aspect** Tolerates full shade. **Soil** Leafy. **Planting partners** *Blechnum penna-marina*, *Ophiopogon planiscapus nigrescens*.

Dog's tooth violet see *Erythronium*

Erythronium

(Dog's tooth violet, trout lily)
Elegant woodland flowers for spring. *E. dens-canis* is the European dog's tooth violet, with pink, white, rose or purple flowers (names like 'Lilac Wonder,' 'Purple King,' 'Rose Queen' and 'Snowflake' are self-explanatory; 'Frans Hals' is violet-pink and 'Charmer' blush pink) on 4in stems over purple-blotched leaves. It will grow in thin grass beneath trees. From North America come the taller trout lilies with marbled leaves, *E. revolutum* with pink, reflexed flowers, the deepest coloring in the Johnsonii group, and *E. californicum* with bronzed foliage and ivory flowers marked with rust and yellow at their hearts. *E. tuolumnense* has heads of lemon yellow flowers over plain green leaves. Hybrids include the exquisite 'White Beauty' with recurved milky petals, sulphur-yellow 'Pagoda' and 'Kondo,'

Erythronium 'Citronella'

and 'Citronella' with wide nodding petals of soft citron, green-tinted on the exterior. *E. americanum* is a dwarf species with rich yellow, purple-spotted flowers. All have corms that must not dry out while dormant.
Size H: 4–8in; S: 6in. **Aspect** Dappled shade. **Soil** Leafy. **Planting partners** *Trillium*, *Anemone nemorosa*.

Fritillaria
(Fritillary)

Most fritillaries prefer an open position, but a few grow well in light shade. *F. pallidiflora* has soft lemon flowers, shaped like angular tulips, on 1ft stems in spring. *F. verticillata* has whorled leaves and wide, pale jade bells on 2ft stems, while *F. involucrata*'s green bells are checkered with terra-cotta to maroon. *F. pontica* has green lanterns tipped with brown, on 1ft stems, and *F. pyrenaica* has mahogany bells with gold interiors. The taller *F. acmopetala* has green bells with mahogany inner segments. The snake's head lily, *F. meleagris*, is a plant of damp meadows but will grow in thin grass beneath trees where the soil is moist; it varies from the checkered red-purple to deep, dusky purple at one extreme and pure white at the other. The last fritillary to flower, in early summer, is *F. camtschatcensis*, a woodlander with green, whorled leaves and near-black bells on 1½ft stems.
Size H: 8in–2ft; S: 6in–1ft. **Aspect** Light shade. **Soil** Moist to well-drained, leafy. **Planting partners** *Arisaema*, *Tricyrtis*.

Galanthus
(Snowdrop)

Most snowdrops grow well in light shade; when well-suited, *G. nivalis* and its double form spread fast to carpet copses with white. Collectors of variant forms have named dozens with minute differences; non-specialists are likely to be content with just a few, such as 'S. Arnott' with large, beautifully formed flowers, 'Magnet' with its flowers swaying on long pedicels, or the very early *G. × atkinsii*. Other species include *G. plicatus* with leaves pleated back at the edge and large, well-marked flowers; *G. elwesii* with broad, glaucous leaves folded together, and large flowers with dark green markings; and *G. ikariae*, flowering a little later and with green leaves. Choice doubles include the tightly rosetted 'Hippolyta' and 'Desdemona' and frail, yellow-marked 'Lady Elphinstone.'
Size H: 6in; S: 4in. **Aspect** Part-shade. **Soil** Any reasonable garden soil. **Planting partners** *Eranthis hyemalis*, *Cyclamen coum*.

Lilium
(Lily)

The martagon lily, *Lilium martagon*, bears its Turk's cap flowers on 3ft stems in early summer. It has an exquisite white variety, *L. martagon* var. *album*, and one with very dark maroon flowers opening from white-furred buds, *L. martagon* var. *cattaniae*. Another easy though less refined lily for shade is *L. pyrenaicum*, which will grow in grass; it forms leafy clumps

Fritillaria meleagris

The bulbs of the shady garden span the seasons, from the snowdrops and Cyclamen coum *of winter and the trout lilies of spring to the true lilies of summer and the fall's* Cyclamen hederifolium.

topped by yellow or rust-red, heavily fragrant Turk's cap flowers.
Size H: 3ft; S: 8in–1½ft. **Aspect** Part-shade. **Soil** Any well-drained garden soil. **Planting partners** *Paeonia*, *Hydrangea*.

Snowdrop see *Galanthus*

Trout lily see *Erythronium*

109

Perennials

Actaea
(Baneberry)

The baneberries have finely cut foliage and insignificant flowers; they are grown above all for their spikes of showy fruit in the fall. *A. alba* (syn. *A. pachypoda*) has white berries on fleshy red stalks on stems of 3ft. *A. rubra* has polished red fruits and *A. spicata* gleaming black, growing to 1½ft. *A. erythrocarpa* bears smaller, wine-red berries on 2½ft stems. All are poisonous.

Size H: 1½ft–3ft; S: 1–1½ft. **Aspect** Tolerates full shade. **Soil** Moist. **Planting partners** *Gentiana asclepiadea*, *Tricyrtis hirta*.

Anemone nemorosa
(Wood anemone)

Garden variants include: white–'Leeds' Variety,' large flowers with faint pink flush; 'Wilks' Giant,' extra-large pure

Corydalis cashmeriana

white; 'Hilda,' small many-petaled flowers. Pink–'Lismore Pink,' pale pink, dark stems; 'Pentre Pink,' later flowers deep pink aging to red. Doubles–'Bracteata Plena,' many narrow petals often tinted green; 'Alba Plena' and 'Vestal,' full-centered with regular outer petals. Blue–'Lismore Blue,' lavender blue with dark stems and gray reverse; 'Blue Bonnet,' sky blue with gray reverse; 'Robinsoniana,' pale lavender blue with fawn reverse; 'Allenii,' large lavender flower with deep lilac reverse; 'Royal Blue,' speedwell blue with paler reverse; 'Bowles' Purple,' dark buds opening to lavender; 'Hannah Gubbay,' maroon buds opening to purple aging blue. 'Virescens' is an oddity with airy green rosette flowers. Similar to the wood anemones are *A. ranunculoides* in bright yellow, single or double ('Flore Pleno'), and *A. × lipsiensis* (*A. nemorosa × A. ranunculoides*) in primrose yellow. All have running roots and dainty foliage, and reach a height of about 4–6in.

Size H: 4–6in; S: 1ft. **Aspect** Part or dappled shade. **Soil** Any leafy soil. **Planting partners** *Narcissus cyclamineus*, *Primula* 'Guinevere.'

Baneberry see *Actaea*

Bergenia

Bold leaves and early spring flowers characterize these tough plants that will grow in any soil. *B. cordifolia* has large green leaves and light mauve-pink flowers; 'Purpurea' is superior, with magenta flowers on red, 2½ft

stems and leaves that color in winter. *B. crassifolia* has spoon-shaped leaves turning maroon in winter, and mauve-pink flowers on 1ft stems. *B. stracheyi* is a miniature of 10in, with rounded leaves and heads of white or pink flowers. Hybrids include 'Bressingham White' and 'Silberlicht' (white); 'Bressingham Bountiful' and 'Bressingham Salmon' (clear pink); 'Abendglut' (semi-double magenta-crimson); 'Morgenrote' (deep pink, repeat-blooming in summer); 'Ballawley' (crimson flowers, glossy leaves –Ballawley hybrids are more readily available); 'Sunningdale' (bright pink flowers, leaves maroon in winter). The varieties that color in winter need full light for the richest tones. *B. ciliata* is more tender and the large, furry leaves may be damaged by frost although the roots are hardy.

Size H: 10in–2½ft; S: 1–2ft. **Aspect** Tolerates full shade. **Soil** Any. **Planting partners** *Iris foetidissima* 'Variegata,' *Dicentra*.

Black-eyed Susan
see *Rudbeckia fulgida*

Cardamine
(Toothwort, lady's smock)

The toothworts and lady's smocks are easy spring-flowering perennials for cool soil. *C. enneaphyllos* bears primrose-cream flowers on 6in stems over lightly bronzed foliage. *C. kitaibelii* also has pale yellow flowers, and whorls of green, pinnate leaves. *C. heptaphylla* (syn. *Dentaria pinnata*) has fresh green divided leaves and pure white flowers on 1½ft stems. *C. pratensis* is the cuckoo flower of damp meadows; the double 'Flore Pleno' has the same lilac coloring and grows to 10in. *C. pentaphyllos* (syn. *Dentaria digitata*) has lilac-pink flowers, and *C. raphanifolia* (syn. *C. latifolia*) has lavender flowers on 1½ft stems. For ground-cover there is *C. trifolia* which has dark, evergreen trefoil leaves and small pure white flowers growing on 6in stems.

Size H: 6in–1½ft; S: 6in–1ft. **Aspect** Part-shade. **Soil** Moist. **Planting partners** *Uvularia*, *Primula vulgaris* 'Schneekissen.'

Celandine see *Ranunculus ficaria*

Christmas rose see *Helleborus*

Convallaria majalis
(Lily-of-the-valley)

This favorite plant with sweet-scented white bells in spring is said to need cool leafy soil but may equally well thrive in clay or push its way into the hard soil of a path. 'Fortin's Giant' extends the season by two weeks. Choice, and less invasive, forms include the pink *rosea*, the double white 'Prolificans,' and 'Albostriata,' its leaves striped with pale yellow.

Size H: 8in; S: 6in–1½ft. **Aspect** Part-shade. **Soil** Any that is not water-logged. **Planting partners** *Hosta*, *Polygonatum*.

Corydalis

C. lutea is a pretty weed with dainty green foliage and clear yellow spurred flowers, ideal for the crevices of a shady wall, growing to 1ft. *C. ochroleuca* is more refined, with ivory flowers over gray-green leaves, and *C. cheilanthifolia* has filigree bronzed foliage and dense sprays of yellow flowers to 6in. They all seed around if contented. Some species are more challenging: *C. cashmeriana* and *C. ambigua* in azure blue, and the brick-pink form of *C. solida* (itself an easy plant with mauve flowers) called 'George P. Baker.'

Size H: 6in–1ft; S: 4in–1½ft. **Aspect** Part-shade. **Soil** Cool, leafy. **Planting partners** *Meconopsis*, *Gentiana* (match for vigor).

Day lily see *Hemerocallis*

Epimedium

Indispensable perennials for shady places, with attractive foliage and dainty flowers, often spurred, in spring. Most form excellent ground-cover. Evergreen species include *E. perralderianum*, with polished leaves and yellow flowers on 1½ft stems; *E. pinnatum colchicum*, with leaves bronzed in winter, and yellow, spurless flowers; *E. × perralchicum* with large yellow flowers; and *E. × cantabrigiense*, with small red and yellow flowers. The deciduous species often display varied tints of spring foliage; they include *E. alpinum*, with red and yellow flowers on 8in stems, and its offspring *E. × ru-*

Actaea pachypoda

From the wildlings of the woodland floor to border perennials, there is a wide choice of flowering and foliage plants, subtle or bold, or brightly colored, for the shady garden.

brum, with crimson flowers over red-tinted leaves; and *E. × versicolor*, with soft yellow-flowered 'Sulphureum' and 'Neosulphureum,' coppery 'Cupreum' and pink 'Versicolor.' *E. × warleyense* has orange flowers. The finest flowers belong to *E. grandiflorum* and its cultivars, 'Crimson Beauty,' 'Rose Queen,' 'White Queen' and the lovely *violaceum*, which all reach 1ft. *E. × youngianum* reaches only 8in and comes in pink-mauve ('Roseum') and white ('Niveum').

Size H: 8in–1½ft; S: 1–1½ft. **Aspect** Part-shade. **Soil** Any good garden soil. **Planting partners** *Corydalis ochroleuca*, ferns.

Gentiana asclepiadea

Ferns

The indispensable furnishings of a shady garden, ranging from the bold blades of the hart's tongue fern, *Phyllitis scolopendrium*, and its variants with wavy or goffered edges, 'Undulatum' and 'Crispum,' to the airy lace of *Athyrium filix-femina*, the lady fern, or the ruffled fronds of the soft shield fern, *Polystichum setiferum*. A baker's dozen of this author's favorite ferns, from among a very long list, would be: *Adiantum pedatum*, a dainty maidenhair fern with black stems to 1½ft; *Athyrium niponicum* var. *pictum*, the Japanese painted fern, with divided, 2ft, glaucous-gray fronds flushed maroon, on maroon stems; *Blechnum tabulare* with bold, hard-textured fronds, coppery-tinted in new growth, reaching 3ft; *Cystopteris bulbifera* with soft, much-divided bright green fronds to 1½ft, bearing tiny bulbils that grow into new plants; *Dryopteris affinis*, the golden-scaled male fern, and the similar *D. wallichiana*, both bold and beautiful with young fronds like golden croziers in spring, unfurling to 5ft; *Matteuccia struthiopteris*, the ostrich plume fern, a moisture-loving, root-traveling species with bold green shuttlecocks to 3ft; *Onoclea sensibilis*, the sensitive fern, lettuce-green with broad segments to the fronds and running roots loving moisture, reaching 2ft; *Osmunda regalis*, the moisture-demanding royal fern, with bold yet elegant green fronds, coppery when young, unfurling to 4ft; *Polypodium vulgare* 'Cornubiense,' a much-divided variant of the tough and tolerant polypody, fresh green even in late summer, growing to 1ft; *Polystichum aculeatum*, the evergreen hard shield fern, with polished green fronds to 3ft; *P. munitum*, the Christmas fern, also known (like some *Nephrolepis* species, which are frost-tender) as sword fern, with glossy, evergreen, radiating, curved fronds to 3ft; forms of *P. setiferum* such as 'Pulcherrimum Bevis,' with dissected fronds sharply narrowed at the tips of the divisions, and the Plumoso-Divisilobum group, with fronds so much divided that they look like moss—both these forms making fronds up to 3ft long; and *Woodwardia radicans*, slightly frost-tender, with fronds to 6ft, arching, clear green, incisively cut, and rooting down at the tips if pegged down.

Size H: 6in–6ft; S: 6in–3ft. **Aspect** Tolerate full shade. **Soil** Leafy. **Planting partners** *Hosta*, *Polygonatum*.

Gentiana asclepiadea
(Willow gentian)

The willow gentian is an undemanding perennial up to 3ft tall, suitable for any moist soil and able to hold its own among shrubs. The arching, leafy stems bear sheaves of ultramarine-blue trumpets in the fall. 'Knightshayes' is pure blue with a white throat and 'Phyllis' sky blue; *alba* is an exquisite white.

Size H: 3ft; S: 2ft. **Aspect** Part-shade. **Soil** Moist. **Planting partners** *Kirengeshoma palmata*, *Actaea*.

Gladwyn iris see *Iris foetidissima*

Haberlea

Hardy gesneriads for shady rocks and walls (see also *Ramonda*). *H. rhodopensis* and *H. ferdinandi-coburgii* both form flat rosettes of toothed, dark green leaves and bear asymmetrical flowers in late spring. The first is typically lilac; its white form, 'Virginalis,' has green-throated flowers. The second has larger flowers, gaping wider, of lilac flecked with yellow in the throat, on 4in stems.

Size H: 4in; S: 6in. **Aspect** Full shade. **Soil** Cool. **Planting partners** *Adiantum pedatum aleuticum*, *Dicentra cucullaria*.

Helleborus

(Christmas rose, Lenten rose)

H. niger is the Christmas rose, its wide white flowers appearing in winter on 12in stems. The earliest of the Lenten rose types is *H. atrorubens*, its half-nodding, maroon-red flowers held on 1½ft stems. Also winter-flowering is *H. foetidus*, of which the most desirable forms are scented, their perfume carrying on the cold air. The black-green leaves are boldly fingered, topped by sheaves of small green bells edged with maroon. Mr. Bowles's Italian form is especially fine, and 'Wester Flisk' has red-stemmed, gray-flushed leaves. Less common in gardens are those with larger, bowl-shaped, green flowers: fragrant *H. cyclophyllus*, *H. dumetorum*, *H. multifidus bocconei* from Italy, *H. multifidus multifidus* with leaves slashed into ribbon segments, and *H. viridis*, which lasts into summer. The Corsican hellebore, *H. argutifolius*, is almost shrubby, with hard, grayish, tooth-edged leaves and thick-stemmed clusters of green, nodding cups in spring; *H. lividus* is similar but exquisitely flushed with pink and dove-gray, and more frost-tender. A group of hybrids with blood of these and *H. niger* are choice and beautiful: *H. × nigercors* with wide, alabaster-green flowers, *H. × sternii*, which combines the hardiness of the Corsican hellebore with the colors of *H. lividus*, and *H. × nigristern*. The Lenten roses of early spring, *H. orientalis*, are very variable, and there are many forms available either according to color or as named cultivars. They range from white (with or without dark freckling inherited from *H. orientalis guttatus*) through pale and mid-pinks to plum and almost black, with excursions into primrose yellow (from the Kochii group). The flower form varies from a wide bowl held facing outwards to a nodding, flared-skirt outline, more graceful but less suited to revealing inner markings. In two small species of subfusc coloring, *H. purpursacens* and *H. torquatus*, the exterior of the maroon flowers is flushed with slaty blue.

Size H: 1–2ft; S: 1–3ft. **Aspect** Light to partial shade. **Soil** Any reasonable garden soil. **Planting partners** *Ribes laurifolium*, *Euphorbia amygdaloides rubra*.

Hemerocallis

(Day lily)

The old lemon lily, *H. lilioasphodelus* (syn. *H. flava*) has fragrant trumpets borne in early summer; *H. citrina* opens its citron blooms towards evening. 'Tetrina's Daughter' is a strongly fragrant form of *H. citrina* with creamy, lemon-yellow flowers. For fragrance, yellow-flowered hybrids beat the fancy pinks and deep reds, and the soft or fiery oranges; two well-tried cultivars are 'Marion Vaughn' and 'Hyperion.' Small-flowered day lilies include species such as *H. dumortieri* and *H. middendorfii*, with fragrant, rich yellow flowers opening from mahogany buds in early summer on 2ft stems, and the taller *H. multiflora*, which bears its scented, amber-yellow flowers in branched heads in late summer. Hybrids of this are 'Isis,' 'Golden Chimes' and the sharper lemon 'Corky.' The old tawny day lily, *H. fulva*, has dull brick-orange flowers but its spring foliage is striking, emerging in sharp lemon-green. It has an untidy double-flowered form and a very desirable variant with cream-striped foliage, 'Kwanzo Variegata.' For small spaces there are *H. minor*, with yellow, fragrant trumpets on 1½ft stems in early summer, and the rare, soft orange *H. forrestii*. The large-flowered, short-stemmed 'Stella d'Oro,' in rich gold, is popular for its exceptionally long season of bloom.

Size H and S: 1½ft–3ft. **Aspect** Light shade. **Soil** Any reasonable garden soil. **Planting partners** *Hosta*, *Phlox*.

Himalayan poppy see *Meconopsis*   *Haberlea rhodopensis*

Hosta

Highly fashionable, these foliage plants are invaluable for shady gardens and can be had in all dimensions, from those with thumbnail-sized leaves to huge dinner plates. Those with puckered leaves, such as *H. sieboldiana* and *H. tokudama*, should not be grown under trees as they collect rubbish on the leaf surface. Here there is only space to pick a score or so from the many hundreds available, grouped according to leaf size.

Large: 'Krossa Regal,' with pointed upstanding leaves white-glaucous beneath, lilac flowers on 6ft stems ('Snowden' is similar); 'Shade Fanfare,' green edged with cream; *H. sieboldiana*, leaves 1ft or more wide, gray-green or glaucous–especially in *H. sieboldiana* var. *elegans*–barely topped by short stems of lilac-white flowers; cultivars of *H. sieboldiana* origin with blue leaves include 'Big Daddy' and 'Blue Umbrellas'; 'Sum and Substance,' green-gold; 'Wide Brim,' blue-green broadly margined with creamy yellow.

Medium: *H. crispula*, dark green broadly margined with white, pale lilac flowers on 2½ft stems in early summer; *H. fortunei albopicta*, yellow edged with green, maturing to pale and dark green, lilac flowers on 2½ft stems in summer; *H. fortunei aureomarginata* ('Obscura Marginata'), green edged with creamy yellow; *H. fortunei hyacinthina*, gray-green edged with gray, good lilac flowers; 'Francee,' deep green edged with white, lavender flowers on 2ft stems in late summer; 'Frances Williams,' primrose-margined form of *H. sieboldiana*; 'Hal-

cyon,' very blue leaves, pale lilac flowers on 1½ft stems in summer; 'Royal Standard,' rich green leaves and fragrant lilac-white flowers on 3ft stems in late summer, superior to 'Honeybells'; 'Tall Boy,' fresh green leaves and striking deep lilac flowers on 5ft stems in summer; 'Thomas Hogg,' dark green edged with ivory, lilac flowers on 2ft stems in early summer; *H. tokudama aureonebulosa*, cupped, deeply corrugated blue leaves marbled with primrose and lime; *H. ventricosa* 'Aureomarginata,' dark glossy green edged with yellow, deep lilac flowers on 4ft stems in late summer. Small: 'Blue Moon,' deeply ribbed glaucous-blue; 'Hydon Sunset,' lime yellow; *H. lancifolia*, pointed, glossy, deep green leaves and lilac flowers on 2ft stems in late summer; *H. minor*, green twisted leaves, violet flowers on 8in stems in late summer; *H. tardiflora*, glossy dark green leaves, large deep lilac flowers on 1ft stems in the fall; *H. venusta*, similar to *H. minor* but even smaller.

Narrow-leaved: 'Ginko Craig,' green margined with white; 'Ground Master,' light green broadly margined with white; *H. rohdeifolia albopicta*, narrowly oblong green leaves broadly margined with yellow; *H. undulata undulata*, very wavy or twisted leaves with broad white central stripe, rich lilac flowers on 1½ft stems in early summer.

Size H: 6in–5ft; S: 8in–3ft. **Aspect** Part-shade. **Soil** Moisture-retentive. **Planting partners** *Astilbe*, ferns in variety.

Iris foetidissima
(Gladwyn iris)

Most irises prefer full sun, though the Pacific Coast hybrids, with their butterfly-like flowers, seem content in light shade, in free-draining soil. The one truly shade-tolerant species is the Gladwyn iris, which has tough-textured evergreen leaves and insignificant flowers followed by pods filled with bright orange seeds. 'Citrina' has superior flowers of clear yellow and mauve and very large seed pods; 'Variegata' is a first-rate evergreen plant with cream-striped leaves but no flowers or seeds. The leaf blades grow to 1½ft.

Size H: 1½ft; S: 2ft. **Aspect** Tolerates full shade. **Soil** Any. **Planting partners** *Bergenia*, *Helleborus*.

Kirengeshoma palmata

A Japanese perennial growing to 3ft, with handsome, plane-like leaves on dark, arching stems, and yellow shuttlecock flowers in the fall.

Size H: 3ft; S: 2ft. **Aspect** Part-shade. **Soil** Moist, lime-free. **Planting partners** *Gentiana asclepiadea*, *Hosta fortunei aureomarginata*.

Lady's smock see *Cardamine*

Lenten rose see *Helleborus*

Lily-of-the-valley
see *Convallaria majalis*

Lungwort see *Pulmonaria*

Meconopsis

(Himalayan poppy)

The genus, virtually restricted to the cool climate of the Pacific Northwest, includes the blue poppies *M. betonicifolia* (which has an albino form), and the massive *M. grandis*, of which GS600 is exceptionally fine. Hybrids of the same pure ultramarine include *M. × sheldonii* and its cultivars or selections, 'Slieve Donard,' the Crewdson hybrids, and the massive 'Branklyn,' with flowers up to 8in wide on 5ft stems. Of the same style but in ivory, not blue, is *M. × sarsonii*. The exquisite harebell poppy, *M. quintuplinervia*, has nodding, lavender-blue flowers on 1½ft stems in spring. Several species have yellow flowers: *M. dhwojii*, beautiful in filigree, bristly, blue-gray leaf; *M. regia*, with nodding primrose saucers over 3ft rosettes of golden-haired leaves; *M. integrifolia*, with huge lampshades of yellow silk up to 1ft wide. All these are monocarpic, that is, they flower and die. Perennial yellow species include the dainty *M. chelidonifolia*, with cut leaves like the greater celandine and sprays of small yellow flowers on 4ft stems, and *M. villosa*, which bears its lemon flowers on 2ft stems in spring over rosettes of leaves furred with amber hairs. The commonest is the Welsh poppy, *M. cambrica*, in yellow or tangerine.

Size H: 1–5ft; S: 1ft–2ft. **Aspect** Part-shade. **Soil** Moist, well-drained, lime-free. **Planting partners** *Primula sikkimensis*, azaleas.

Nicotiana

(Tobacco flower)

N. sylvestris is a giant among tobacco flowers, forming piles of sticky, soft green leaves up to 3ft wide, topped by huge open spires up to 6ft tall of long-tubed, white trumpets, emitting an intense sweet perfume especially at night. Overwintered plants begin to flower from mid-summer. In mild areas the green-flowered *N. langsdorfii* may survive the winter; it reaches 3ft, and has small, wide-mouthed trumpets with azure-blue anthers. The familiar, though often scentless, bedding tobacco flowers also thrive in shade.

Size H: 2–6ft; S: 2–3ft. **Aspect** Light shade. **Soil** Any reasonable garden soil. **Planting partners** *Veratrum*, *Hemerocallis*.

Paeonia

(Peony)

Most peonies do best in open places, but some appreciate shelter from wind and scorching sun. Among them are the tongue-twisting *P. mlokosewitschii*, with pink-tinted young growth and fleeting lemon cups in spring; the larger-flowered, paler *P. wittmanniana*, which also reaches 2ft in flower; and the exquisite *P. obovata alba* in white, and *P. obovata willmottiae* in palest lemon, over glaucous and bronze leaves, growing to 1½ft. All these can be raised from seed: red seeds are infertile, blue or black ones fertile. The *P. wittmanniana* hybrid 'Mai Fleuri' has bronzed and mahogany young growth and cream, faintly

blushed flowers. Others spread, slowly or quite fast, at the root: *P. mascula arietina* with magenta-pink flowers and grayish foliage, of which 'Northern Glory' is a superb form growing to 2½ft; the shorter *P. mollis* in vivid magenta with gray-lilac leaves; *P. tenuifolia* with very finely cut leaves and deep crimson flowers on 1½ft stems; and *P. peregrina* in scarlet–cultivars are the very bright 'Fire King' and salmon-scarlet 'Sunshine'; all grow to 2ft. *P. veitchii woodwardii* has fresh green foliage and soft pink flowers on 1ft stems; it is variable–the best with large flowers–from seed, and does not run at the root.

Size H: 1½–2½ft; S: 2ft. **Aspect** Light shade. **Soil** Any reasonable garden soil. **Planting partners** *Narcissus*, *Lilium*.

Kirengeshoma palmata

Primula
× *pruhonicensis*
'Marie Crousse'

Podophyllum

(Umbrella leaf)

A small genus of herbaceous perennials whose common name describes their curious foliage, which pushes shiny snouts through the soil in spring to unfurl into glossy, lobed leaves folded from the top of the stem like an umbrella. *P. hexandrum* (syn. *P. emodi*) has upright white to pink flowers above the foliage in spring and shiny red fruits shaped like a plum tomato; *P. hexandrum* var. *chinense* has larger, pink flowers. *P. peltatum* is the North American May apple, with one or two leaves to each stem, and nodding white flowers followed by light red fruits. Both species stand 1½ft tall at maturity, and can easily be raised from seed sown as soon as it is ripe.

Size H: 1½ft; S: 1ft. **Aspect** Part-shade. **Soil** Moist. **Planting partners** Ferns, *Mahonia*.

Polygonatum

(Solomon's seal)

The common *P.* × *hybridum* is an easy shade plant with the arching stems typical of the genus; hanging, narrow, alabaster-white bells open in late spring. It has a cultivar with cream-striped leaves, 'Striatum.' *P. biflorum* is twice as tall, at 5ft, and another tall one is *P. verticillatum*, different in style with upright stems and whorls of narrow leaves. *P. odoratum*, with angled stems up to 2ft, is fragrant, and comes in various forms: double 'Flore Pleno' and the cream-striped 'Variegatum' among them. *P. falcatum* is only half as tall, with leafy stems and ivory bells in late spring; 'Variegatum' has leaves margined with white and tinged with pink.

Size H: 1–3ft; S: 1–1½ft. **Aspect** Part-shade. **Soil** Leafy. **Planting partners** Ferns, *Hosta*.

Primula

(Primula, primrose)

The common primrose, with its pale flowers, has given rise to several color forms, and other species have entered the fray to enrich the range and add differing leaf forms and growth habits. Few of the named kinds are easy to keep, needing moist soil rich in organic matter and frequent division: they are collectors' pieces. Easy kinds of primrose or polyanthus type include the Garryarde primrose 'Guinevere,' with bronzed leaves and lilac-pink flowers; *P. vulgaris* var. *sibthorpii* with pale mauve flowers; and 'Groeneken's Glory' in brighter lilac. 'Schneekissen' is white and 'Blue Riband' deep blue with a yellow eye. The old doubles, lilac 'Lilacina Plena' or 'Quaker's Bonnet' and white 'Alba Plena,' are more tricky. Primroses with the blood of *P. juliae* are generally easier; bright magenta 'Wanda' is almost indestructible, it seems. 'Tawny Port' is more demanding, with dark leaves and deep burgundy flowers; 'Kinlough Beauty' is small and dainty, with pink, candy-striped flowers, as are the miniature polyanthuses 'Lady Greer' and 'McWatt's Cream,' both in palest primrose. Doubles include rosy-mauve, white-splashed 'Marie Crousse' and 'Our Pat,' with dark leaves and deep violet flowers. 'Sue Jervis' is a peach-pink double that seems easy. Seed selections include the eyeless Cowichans in a range of rich colors, and the gold- and silver-laced polyanthus, each petal finely rimmed with yellow or white on a dark red ground. Oddities such as hose-in-hose (one flower within another) and Jack-in-the-greens, with a ruff of green leaves around the flower, sometimes crop up among seedlings.

Size H and S: 4–6in. **Aspect** Part-shade. **Soil** Moist, rich, well-drained. **Planting partners** *Viola odorata*, *Dodecatheon*.

Pulmonaria

(Lungwort)

The lungworts are undemanding perennials for shade, flowering from earliest spring. One of the first is *P. rubra*, which has plain green leaves and coral-red flowers on 6in stems. Selected forms include 'Bowles' Red' and 'Redstart,' a white, and 'Barfield

Pink.' The leaves of *P. officinalis* bear white spots and the flowers open bright pink and fade to lilac-blue, giving rise to the alternative names of Joseph and Mary or soldiers and sailors. There is a good white, 'Sissinghurst White,' and selections of purer blue, 'Bowles' Blue' and 'Cambridge.' In leaf *P. saccharata* can be much more striking, often so boldly blotched as to be almost wholly silvered, as in *P. saccharata argentea*. 'Mrs Moon' is another good selection, and 'Leopard' is heavily spotted, with pink flowers. The related *P. vallarsae* 'Margery Fish' is heavily spotted with platinum.

The diminutive *P. angustifolia*, with plain green leaves, bears sprays of ultramarine flowers in early spring: *P. angustifolia azurea*, 'Mawson's Blue' and 'Munstead Blue' are named forms. Appealing in both flower and leaf, *P. longifolia* has long, narrow, silver-spotted leaves and small flowers of pure deep blue in late spring on 8in stems. 'Bertram Anderson' has flowers nearer to violet.

The giant of the genus is *P. mollis*, with deep blue flowers fading towards purple, on 1½ft stems, and large, velvety, green leaves. For the best foliage, cut lungworts hard back after flowering and give them a feed and a good soaking; new fresh leaves will grow and last all summer.
Size H: 4in–1½ft; S: 6in–2ft. **Aspect** Part-shade. **Soil** Any reasonable garden soil. **Planting partners** *Dicentra*, small daffodils.

Ramonda

Another genus of hardy gesneriads. *R. myconi* has flat rosettes of dark green, wrinkled leaves, and rounded lavender-blue flowers with yellow centers in spring. *R. myconi* 'Rosea' is pink. *R. nathaliae* is similar, with glossier leaves, and has an enchanting white form. *R. serbica* has smaller flowers of more cupped outline. All reach 4in in flower, and like best to grow in vertical crevices in rocks out of the sun.
Size H: 4in; S: 6in. **Aspect** Full shade. **Soil** Cool. **Planting partners** *Adiantum pedatum aleuticum*, *Dicentra cucullaria*.

Ranunculus ficaria
(Celandine)

The common celandine can be a bad weed, but its garden forms are collectors' pieces of great charm, without invasive tendencies. Single-flowered cultivars include 'Brazen Hussy' with glossy, almost black leaves and shining yellow flowers; *R. ficaria cupreus* with gleaming copper flowers and *citrinus* in pale lemon; *R. ficaria albus* in white, surpassed by 'Salmon's White' with broad ivory petals and a pale yellow central boss; 'Primrose' with large, ample flowers. There are several doubles: *R. ficaria flore pleno*, lemon with a green center; 'Picton's Double,' a full pompom of clear yellow; 'E. A. Bowles' with satiny lemon petals; 'Collarette' with a tight center and neat yellow frill; a double cream with dusky reverse to the petals; a double bronze.
Size H: 3in; S: 4in. **Aspect** Part-

shade. **Soil** Any reasonable garden soil. **Planting partners** *Hacquetia epipactis*, *Hepatica*.

Rudbeckia fulgida
(Black-eyed Susan)

Cheerful yellow daisies with a bold black central cone, more the sort of thing you would expect in a sunny border, but 2ft *R. fulgida sullivantii* 'Goldsturm' flowers freely in shady places in sticky, damp soils.
Size H: 2ft; S: 1ft. **Aspect** Light shade. **Soil** Moist. **Planting partners** *Crocosmia*, *Hemerocallis*.

Smilacina racemosa
(False spikenard)

A relative of Solomon's seal, this has similar foliage, but the flowers are frothy, creamy, fragrant spikes in late spring, on 2½ft stems. Said to dislike lime.
Size H: 2½ft; S: 2ft. **Aspect** Part-shade. **Soil** Prefers lime-free. **Planting partners** *Dicentra*, *Paeonia*.

Solomon's seal see *Polygonatum*

Toad lily see *Tricyrtis*

Tobacco flower see *Nicotiana*

Toothwort see *Cardamine*

Tricyrtis
(Toad lily)

The toad lilies bear their bizarre, often mottled flowers in late summer and fall. *T. formosana* Stolonifera group increases freely at the roots, and bears dark green leaves; the branching, 2–3ft stems bear dark buds opening to brown, mauve-spotted flowers. The earliest to flower, in summer, is *T. latifolia* (syn. *T. bakeri*), with ocher-yellow flowers flecked with purple and mottled leaves; the later *T. macropoda*, also about 3ft tall, has creamy-green flowers with mauve spotting. *T. hirta* has large white flowers heavily blotched and spotted with purple, or entirely white. 'White Towers' has softly furred leaves and milk-white flowers. Some species have soft yellow, shuttlecock flowers: *T. macrantha* and its variety *macranthopsis*, with sheaves of arching stems and nodding flowers, and *T. ohsumiensis* with up-facing, open flowers.
Size H and S: 1–3ft. **Aspect** Part-shade. **Soil** Leafy. **Planting partners** *Actaea*, *Fritillaria*.

Trillium

The wake robin is *T. grandiflorum*, with pure white three-part flowers over plain green leaves; it has a pretty double form. *T. ovatum* is similar, flushing pink with age. The very variable *T. erectum* ranges from white to dusky red via pink, green and yellow. *T. luteum* is also yellow, washed with green, over mottled leaves, resembling *T. sessile*, which also has prick-eared flowers, rich maroon, pink or white.

T. chloropetalum also resembles this. Tiny trilliums for shady rocks or raised beds include *T. rivale*, with white or blush maroon-spotted flowers, the prairie trillium, *T. recurvatum*, with mottled leaves and toad-colored flowers, and the painted trillium, *T. undulatum*, with a bold crimson stripe at the base of each pink petal. The smallest, *T. nivale*, the snow trillium, has very early, pure white flowers.
Size H: 4in–2ft; S: 6in–1ft. **Aspect** Part-shade. **Soil** Leafy, lime-free. **Planting partners** *Erythronium*, *Mertensia virginica*.

Veratrum

Herbaceous perennials with bold, poisonous pleated leaves and spires of close-packed, tiny flowers. *V. nigrum* has the noblest leaves, and very dark maroon flowers on 5ft stems. *V. album* has smaller leaves but, in its best forms, great plumes of ivory flowers in summer. *V. viride* has less striking, green flowers.
Size H: 5ft; S: 2ft. **Aspect** Part-shade. **Soil** Moist, rich. **Planting partners** *Hosta*, ferns.

Umbrella leaf see *Podophyllum*

Viola
(Violet)

The sweet violets and their scentless cousins fill shady corners in any reasonable soil. Forms of *V. odorata* range from the familiar violet-blue and white

to named selections such as 'Coeur d'Alsace' in pink, azure 'Princess Alexandra,' 'Red Charm,' 'Skimmed Milk' and buff-yellow 'Sulphurea.' 'Czar' is a good purple. The bright yellow-flowered *V. pensylvanica*, *V. glabella* and *V. biflora* are scentless and apt to seed themselves all too freely. Even more rampant are the pink *V. rupestris rosea* and purple-leaved *V. labradorica*, as well as the scentless dog violets with lilac flowers, *V. riviniana* and *V. canina*. All these are best kept among shrubs, where they can cover the ground without choking tiny treasures. Some of the prettiest violets, lacking only scent, are those with wide butterfly blooms: *V. obliqua* (syn. *V. cucculata*), *V. sororia* 'Albiflora,' *V. papilionacea* and *V. septentrionalis*, with blue or white flowers. 'Freckles' is a form with white flowers heavily flecked with violet. Equally valuable in shade, especially among shrubs where it will weave its stems among neighboring branches, is *V. cornuta*, which has wide-open flowers of lavender, white or near-blue. The chinless *V. hederacea* has white and lilac flowers on 3in stems and needs a warm, lightly shaded place.
Size H: 3–6in; S: 6in–1ft. **Aspect** Part-shade. **Soil** Leafy. **Planting partners** Primroses, *Corylopsis*.

Willow gentian
see *Gentian asclepiadea*

Wood anemone
see *Anemone nemorosa*

Shrubs and climbers

Blueberry see *Vaccinium*

Camellia

Camellia × williamsii is the most adaptable of camellias, varying from 'J.C. Williams' with pale pink single flowers to the opulent double 'Debbie' in rich pink. Other singles include deep pink 'St Ewe' and 'November Pink,' which flowers all winter in open weather, pink 'Mary Christian' and white 'Francis Hanger.' These shed their fading flowers cleanly, but not all the doubles do. They include semi-double 'Donation' in mid-pink, 'Elsie Jury' in orchid pink, varying from anemone to peony form, 'Anticipation' with peony-form crimson-pink flowers, and 'Dream Boat,' a formal double pink dropping cleanly when over. *C. sasanqua* and its hybrids are among the hardiest and earliest flowering of the genus. *C.* 'Cornish Snow' is a single white, early and free-flowering, the best landscape white camellia. All camellias need an acid, leafy soil and moisture in summer.
Size H: 6–8ft; S: 4–8ft. **Aspect** Part-shade. **Soil** Moist, lime-free. **Planting partners** *Omphalodes cappadocica*, *Gaultheria*.

Clematis

Many clematis grow and flower well in light shade. The shade gardener's ally above all is spring-flowering *C. montana*, which grows where almost nothing else will. The type is white and smells of vanilla; *C. montana* var.

rubens is pink with bronzed foliage. White-flowered forms include 'Grandiflora' in pure white with no scent, creamy, fragrant 'Alexander,' and chocolate-scented *C. montana* var. *wilsonii*, which flowers a month later. Pale pinks such as 'Elizabeth,' 'Vera,' 'Odorata' and 'Pink Perfection,' all scented, fade to near-white in shade. Deeper pinks are unscented: 'Picton's Variety,' 'Freda,' 'Rubens Superba' and 'Mayleen' all have bronzed foliage. 'Tetrarose' has very large rosy mauve flowers and bronze leaves.
Size H: 30ft; S: 20ft. **Aspect** Tolerates full shade. **Soil** Rich. **Planting partners** *Pinus* (to provide support), *Viburnum plicatum* 'Mariesii.'

Clethra

Clethra delavayi is an aristocratic shrub for sheltered shade, flowering in summer. The long sprays of milk-white bells have brown anthers and gray calyces turning to pink as the petals fall. The leaves are softly hairy beneath. The evergreen, tree-like *C. arborea*, with large white bells like lily-of-the-valley, is only for virtually frost-free gardens.
Size H: 10ft; S: 8ft. **Aspect** Dappled shade. **Soil** Acid, moist. **Planting partners** *Helleborus lividus*, *Athyrium niponicum pictum*.

Corylopsis

Corylopsis pauciflora is a shrub for acid soil and sheltered, dappled shade, bearing cowslip-scented, soft yellow

Rhododendron cinnabarinum

Evergreen shrubs form the framework of the shady garden, flowering shrubs decorate it with color, and climbers add another dimension as they hoist themselves upwards.

flowers in spring just before the new leaves unfurl in shades of coral pink. It grows slowly to about 4ft. Taller and bolder is *C. sinensis calvescens veitchiana*, which tolerates some lime and has showy sprays of lemon-yellow, red-anthered, cowslip-scented flowers. *C. sinensis* 'Spring Purple' has maroon-tinted young foliage and nodding, soft lemon flowers.
Size H and S: 4–6ft. **Aspect** Part-shade. **Soil** Leafy, neutral to acid. **Planting partners** *Anemone apennina*, *Rhododendron thomsonii*.

Cranberry see *Vaccinium*

Daphne odora

Danae racemosa

An elegant evergreen shrub related to butcher's broom, forming sheaves of arching, 3ft stems set with narrow cladodes (flattened stems performing the function of leaves) of shining dark green. Red fruits may form in the fall. **Size** H: 3ft; S: 2ft. **Aspect** Tolerates full shade. **Soil** Moist. **Planting partners** *Daphne odora*, ferns.

Daphne odora

An evergreen shrub with glossy, dark green leaves and clusters of sweetly fragrant flowers in late winter. *D. odora* 'Aureo-marginata' is slightly hardier than *D. odora* and has attractive leaves margined with yellow. **Size** H: 2½ft; S: 3ft. **Aspect** Tolerates full shade. **Soil** Moist, well-drained. **Planting partners** *Epimedium*, ferns.

Fatsia japonica

A large evergreen shrub thriving in shade, ideal in town gardens. It bears bold, fingered, dark green leaves with lightly deckled margins, and heads of creamy flowers revealing its ivy affiliations in the fall. Its size can be restrained by growing it in a container and it lends itself well to arborizing. **Size** H and S: 8ft. **Aspect** Tolerates full shade. **Soil** Any reasonable garden soil. **Planting partners** Bamboos, *Hosta*.

Gaultheria

Ericaceous plants for acid soils. The salal, *G. shallon*, tolerates the densest shade (though it will hardly flower in darkness) but is too rampant for polite company. Better behaved is *G. procumbens*, the wintergreen, forming a dense evergreen carpet set with tiny white flowers that develop into showy red fruits in the fall. Several species have white or blue fruits: among those small enough for raised beds are *G. trichophylla* with tiny leaves, pink flowers and turquoise fruits, *G. cuneata* with white fruits and bronzed leaves, *G. itoana* with white fruits and green leaves, and *G. miqueliana* with white or pink berries. Taller than these are *G. wardii*, with china-blue fruits, *G. hookeri* with turquoise, and indigo-blue *G. semi-infera*. *G. forrestii* has better flowers, white, fragrant urns, followed by deep blue fruits. *G. hispida* is white in flower and fruit. **Size** H: 6in–4ft; S: 6in–3ft. **Aspect** Part-shade. **Soil** Acid. **Planting partners** *Pieris, Leucothoë*.

Hedera

(Ivy)

Ivies vary from tiny, non-climbing or barely creeping forms of *H. helix* to the massive Irish ivy, *H. hibernica*. There are hundreds of cultivars of *H. helix*. Here are just ten: 'Adam,' neat white-variegated leaves flushing pink in winter; 'Congesta' and the similar 'Conglomerata,' dwarf shrubby forms with close-packed leaves on upright stems to 2ft; 'Goldheart,' triangular leaves each with a golden central flash; 'Harald,' green and cream; 'Heron,' with bright green, narrow, five-lobed leaves like a bird's foot; 'Ivalace,' slow and neat with dark green leaves curled at the margins; 'Sagittifolia,' light green, five-lobed leaves, the center lobe very long, the side and base lobes small, and its cream-suffused form 'Sagittifolia Variegata'; 'Shamrock,' compact with dark green, three-lobed, cupped leaves; 'Très Coupé,' tiny, five-lobed leaves like a diminutive 'Sagittifolia.'

Other species include *H. canariensis*, to which belongs the slightly frost-tender 'Gloire de Marengo' with silvery, cream and gray marbled leaves; and *H. colchica*, the Persian ivy, with huge leaves, most striking in the cultivars 'Dentata Variegata,' margined in primrose, and 'Sulphur Heart,' with central primrose markings. **Size** H: 1ft–almost unlimited (as climber, depending on support and variety); S: 1ft–almost unlimited (as ground-cover, depending on variety). **Aspect** Tolerates full shade. **Soil** Any reasonable garden soil. **Planting partners** *Hosta*, ferns.

Hydrangea

The mophead forms of *H. macrophylla* and *H. serrata* are best suited to formal or semi-formal situations and the lacecaps are ideal in woodland or informal shrub borders. One of the finest hydrangeas for shade is *H. aspera villosa* (syn. *H. villosa*), a large shrub with mauve-pink fertile florets and, in the best forms, lavender-blue sterile florets. *H. sargentiana*, with immense, dark green velvety leaves and furred stems, thrives even in dense shade; its hummocky flowers are deep mauve with white sterile florets. *H. quercifolia* has bold, oak-like leaves, which color in the fall. Toughest of all is *H. paniculata*, with white, lacy, dome-shaped inflorescences; 'Praecox,' 'Floribunda' and 'Tardiva' together span several weeks in flower; while 'Grandiflora' has large heavy heads of sterile florets. All except 'Praecox' age towards pink; 'Pink Diamond' shows color from the start. 'Kyushu' has lacy, long-lasting flowers. The climbing hydrangeas, deciduous *H. anomala petiolaris* and evergreen *H. serratifolia*, flower most freely in sun but grow well in light shade; the first bears white lacecap flowers, the second foamy ivory heads in late summer. The related *Schizophragma* species are also self-clinging: *S. hydrangeoides* is deciduous and has a pink form, 'Roseum,' while ivory *S. integrifolium* has bold lacecap flowers. All the climbing hydrangeas and relatives are self-clinging.
Size H and S: 2–8ft. **Aspect** Part-shade. **Soil** Moist, retentive, acid to neutral. **Planting partners** *Astilbe*, Japanese anemones.

Itea ilicifolia

An evergreen shrub for light shade and some shelter, this has dark green, polished leaves like a holly's, but unarmed, and long tassles of fragrant, ivory-green flowers in late summer.
Size H and S: 6ft. **Aspect** Light shade. **Soil** Any reasonable garden soil. **Planting partners** *Azara*, *Pileostegia*.

Ivy see *Hedera*

Leucothoë

A small genus of ericaceous, mostly evergreen shrubs for cool, acid soils in dappled shade. *L. fontanesiana*, which grows to 3ft or so, has arching stems set with pointed, shining green leaves turning to copper in winter, and clusters of white pitcher-shaped flowers along the stems in spring. It has a jazzy variegated form, 'Rainbow,' with leaves marbled pink, cream and yellow on green. Two weeks later the smaller *L. davisiae* opens its upright spikes of white flowers, and later again is the smallest of all, *L. keiskei*, characterized by reddish, zigzag stems and pointed, glossy leaves. It needs moister soil than the others.
Size H and S: 1–3ft. **Aspect** Part-shade. **Soil** Acid. **Planting partners** *Pieris*, *Rhododendron*.

Mahonia

As well as the familiar spring-flowering Oregon grape, *M. aquifolium*, and *M. japonica*, with its pinnate leaves formed of holly-like leaflets and strings of yellow bells scented of lily-of-the-valley in winter, the genus includes low creeping shrubs and the tall, tree-like Himalayan species. *M. nervosa* is a small shrub, which spreads by suckers, with glossy leaflets forming clear-cut patterns. Rather taller is *M. repens rotundifolia*, which has rounded, not spiny leaflets of sea green. Hybrids of *M. aquifolium* include 'Toluacensis,' with narrow, undulate leaflets bronzed in winter, and 'Moseri,' in which the young growths are apricot fading to apple green, maturing to dark green in summer and flushing red in winter. At the other extreme is the lanky *M. lomariifolia*, with ladder-like leaves of many narrow leaflets in big ruffs topping bare stems, and upright candles of yellow flowers. Crosses between this and *M. japonica* are grouped as *M. × media*; one of the best of the group, being fragrant as well as showy, is 'Winter Sun.'
Size H and S: 1ft–8ft. **Aspect** Part-shade. **Soil** Any reasonable garden soil. **Planting partners** Ferns, *Iris foetidissima*.

Pileostegia viburnoides

An evergreen, self-clinging, climbing relative of the hydrangeas with excellent bold, oblong leaves, and pyramids of ivory froth in late summer, most freely borne when it receives sun for part of the day.
Size H and S: 20ft. **Aspect** Tolerates full shade. **Soil** Any reasonable garden soil. **Planting partners** *Fatsia*, *Mahonia*.

Rhododendron

This vast genus encompasses tiny rock garden shrublets and tall trees. What follows is a personal selection; if you become addicted, you will find many books and fellow enthusiasts to lure you on. Species rhododendrons have the greatest charm but may not be the easiest to grow; the old hardy hybrids are tough and easy anywhere in acid soil. Primary hybrids or those of which the parentage is still close to the wild species often combine the best characteristics of species and hybrids: dignity, grace and vigor. The Loderi group mature to tree size, with peeling, pink-marbled bark; the flowers are bold as lilies and strongly fragrant: 'King George' has pale pink buds opening to white, 'Venus' is blush pink and 'White Diamond' pure white. Better suited to small gardens is 'Solidarity,' a wide bush with soft pink-scarlet bells. May Day has waxy scarlet funnels and leaves backed with tan felt. 'Hotei' is a compact shrub with primrose flowers and 'Rothenberg' has clear creamy bells. Hawk Crest is a larger clear yellow. Among blues (always with a hint of lavender or purple) *R. augustinii* is a tall shrub; 'Electra' is a fine form in violet-blue with green flash. *R. cinnabarinum* and its allies all have waxy, narrow bells and glaucous-blue foliage; alas they are susceptible to powdery mildew. Lady Chamberlain is soft terra-cotta, Lady Rosebery pink, 'Conroy' tangerine, 'Bodnant Yellow' warm amber, 'Vin Rosé' wine red and the Concatenans group ocher yellow with very blue leaves.

R. williamsii and its offspring, dome-shaped bushes with rounded leaves bronzed in spring, are ideal for small gardens. *R. williamsii* itself has shell-pink bells, Humming Bird carmine, 'Temple Belle' rosy buds opening to pink, 'Mission Bells' palest pinkish white and Bow Bells cherry-red buds opening to pink. Also for small spaces, 'Patty Bee' is a dwarf hybrid with small yellow tubular flowers in spring; 'Ginny Gee' has numerous, white, pink-tinged flowers. 'Praecox' bears its amethyst-purple funnels in winter; Tessa is smaller, pinker and later to flower, while Seta also bears its white, pink-tipped flowers in early spring.

Rhododendrons with beautiful foliage are year-round shrubs of the highest value. Some have tawny or silvered felting on the reverse of the leaves. Among the easiest of the large-leaved rhododendrons, which need shelter and atmospheric moisture, is *R. hodgsonii*, its dark gleaming green leaves backed with beige felt. *R. macabeanum* has massive, silver-backed leaves unfurling from scarlet-scaled buds, and lemon, tubby bells in spring. The long leaves of *R. falconeri* are rust-red beneath; waxy, creamy flowers are borne in large trusses. Smaller-leaved species with felty leaves include *R. bureavii*, deep green backed fox red; *R. roxieanum* Oreonastes group, with narrow, russet-backed leaves; *R. haematodes* with scarlet bells and dark, tawny-felted leaves; and *R. arboreum* 'Sir Charles Lemon,' with deep brown felting, mahogany stems, and white flowers. *R. thomsonii* has rounded, glaucous-blue leaves and flaking pink bark. *R. lutescens* has citron-yellow flowers among coppery young foliage. *R. oreotrephes* has glaucous-blue foliage and mauve bells; and low, mounded *R. glaucophyllum* has rose-pink bells amid blue-green, white-backed and aromatic leaves. Smaller still is bristly, blue-leaved, yellow-flowered *R. lepidostylum*.

There are several frost-tender species and hybrids with white, lily-like flowers and rich lily perfume, typified by 'Fragrantissimum.' Also suitable for dappled shade are the azaleas. 'Summer Fragrance' is deciduous, with scented, white, primrose-flashed flowers; 'Daviesii' is white and yellow, and soft yellow 'Narcissiflorum' has double flowers. *R. canascens* is the Piedmont azalea, with fragrant white-pink, almost rose, flowers.
Size H and S: 1–20ft. **Aspect** Dappled shade. **Soil** Acid. **Planting partners** *Lilium*, ferns.

Sarcococca

Small evergreen shrubs flowering in winter, hence their common name Christmas box. *S. hookeriana* var. *humilis* is a low shrub, spreading by suckers, with tiny fragrant flowers. Rather larger is *S. ruscifolia*, with red fruits, not black. *S. saligna* is the finest in leaf, but rather frost-tender and not fragrant. For all-round value choose *S. hookeriana* var. *digyna*, with narrow leaves on upright, densely branched, dark red stems and tiny, creamy-blush, honey-fragrant flowers.
Size H and S: 1–2ft. **Aspect** Part-shade. **Soil** Any reasonable garden soil. **Planting partners** *Helleborus*, *Daphne*.

Skimmia

Sometimes said to dislike lime, the skimmias require shade and soil rich in organic matter, when they should remain healthily dark green in leaf. Male plants have the finer flowers, but the females bear showy scarlet berries. *S. japonica* 'Rubella' is a male with rich crimson buds in winter, opening to white flowers in spring; 'Fragrans' (also male) is less showy but smells of lily-of-the-valley. 'Ruby Dome' is a compact, red-budded male. 'Nymans' is a fine berrying cultivar of open growth. For very limited spaces, 'Bowles' Dwarf' comes in both male and female forms. The hybrid *S. × confusa* 'Kew Green' is low and wide-spreading, with bright green, aromatic leaves and pale green flowers in spring.

Size H: 1–6ft; S: 1–5ft. **Aspect** Part-shade. **Soil** Rich, moist, neutral. **Planting partners** *Danae racemosa*, *Ribes laurifolium*.

Vaccinium

(Cranberry, blueberry, whortleberry) A genus of ericaceous shrubs varying from tiny creepers to the familiar blueberry of pies and jellies. The Caucasian whortleberry, *V. arctostaphylos*, is a spreading shrub with clusters of white or red bells in summer followed by shiny black fruits; the large leaves turn to mahogany in the fall and fall in winter. The Madeiran *V. padifolium* is taller, of upright habit, with green bells in summer, while *V. cylindraceum*, from the Azores, is also surprisingly frost-resistant; it bears showy clusters of tubular flowers, red in bud

opening to green and brick-red. *V. floribundum* (syn. *V. mortinia*) is an evergreen shrub with neat, dark leaves, mahogany when young, and dense sprays of pink urn-shaped flowers followed by red fruits. *V. ovatum* is similarly elegant, but taller at 6ft or more. The cranberry, *V. oxycoccos*, and the American cranberry, *V. macrocarpon*, are creepers with edible red fruits; *V. vitis-idaea*, the cowberry, also bears red fruits, most striking in the cultivar 'Koralle.' Most beautiful of the genus is *V. glaucoalbum*, a spreading, 3ft evergreen with large, blue-gray, white-backed leaves and pale pink flowers in silvery-rose bracts in early summer.

Size H: 1in–6ft; S: 1–6ft. **Aspect** Part-shade. **Soil** Acid. **Planting partners** Azaleas, *Leucothoë*.

Viburnum

The lacecap and snowball viburnums, forms of *V. plicatum*, *V. sargentii* and *V. opulus*, do well in light shade in any reasonable soil. For small spaces you could choose *V. plicatum* 'Watanabe.' A few lesser-known species are handsome shrubs for shady places. For acid soils, there are *V. lantanoides* (syn. *V. alnifolium*) and *V. furcatum*, both with bold, broad leaves coloring richly in the fall. *V. henryi* is a lime-tolerant evergreen with narrow, dark, polished leaves, bobbly white cones of flower at mid-summer, and sprays of fruit that age from red to black. Its offspring *V. × hillieri* 'Winton' is hardly less attractive, the broader leaves unfurling in copper tints in spring. All grow to

Zenobia pulverulenta

6ft or more in height and spread.
Size H and S: 6–8ft. **Aspect** Part-shade. **Soil** Any reasonable garden soil (acid for some species). **Planting partners** *Hosta*, *Clematis viticella*.

Whortleberry see *Vaccinium*

Zenobia pulverulenta

An ericaceous shrub with deciduous or semi-evergreen, glaucous foliage, bloomy white young shoots and large white bells, like an opulent lily-of-the-valley but scented of aniseed, in early summer. Remove the flowered stems by cutting them back to strong new shoots, or it will soon begin to look scruffy. It can be raised from seed but not all the seedlings will be as blue-bloomy as the best forms.

Size H and S: 3ft. **Aspect** Part-shade. **Soil** Acid. **Planting partners** *Leucothoë*, *Pieris*.

Index

Page numbers in *italics* refer to illustrations; numbers in **bold** to the chapter on Key Plants.

Plant hardiness zones

This hardiness map will help you to establish which plants are most suitable for your garden. The zones 2–11 are based on the average annual minimum temperature for each zone and appear after the plant entry in the index. The lower number indicates the northernmost zone in which the plant can survive the winter, and the higher number, the most southerly area in which it will perform consistently. Plants marked * are only suitable for the West Coast and rhododendrons marked ** are only suitable for coastal California. Plant zones 2–3 are suitable for central Canada and zones 4–6 are suitable for coastal and southern Canada.

ZONE 2	−50° TO −40° F
ZONE 3	−40° TO −30°
ZONE 4	−30° TO −20°
ZONE 5	−20° TO −10°
ZONE 6	−10° to 0°
ZONE 7	0° TO 10°
ZONE 8	10° TO 20°
ZONE 9	20° TO 30°
ZONE 10	30° TO 40°
ZONE 11	ABOVE 40°

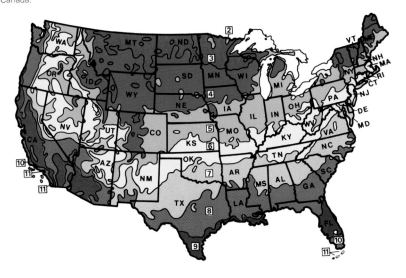

Acknowledgments

The publisher thanks the following photographers and organizations for their kind permission to reproduce the photographs in this book:

1 Michael Boys/Boys Syndication; 2–3 IPC Magazines/Robert Harding Picture Library; 4–5 Elizabeth Whiting and Associates; 6–7 Marijke Heuff (Mr. & Mrs. Poley-Bom, Holland); 8 Jacqui Hurst/Boys Syndication; 9 Marijke Heuff (Garden Mien Ruys); 10 Andrew Lawson; 11 above Philippe Perdereau; 11 below Marijke Heuff (Mrs. L Koeg Amerlaan, Holland); 12–3 Gary Rogers; 14 Peter Woloszynski; 15 Philippe Perdereau; 16 left Jerry Harpur/Elizabeth Whiting and Associates; 16 right Philippe Perdereau; 17 Philippe Perdereau; 19 Elizabeth Whiting and Associates; 21 Michael Boys/Boys Syndication; 22 Hugh Palmer; 23 Michael Boys/Boys Syndication; 24 Photos Horticultural; 25 Marijke Heuff; 26 Marijke Heuff (Mr. & Mrs. Voornijk-Luca, Holland); 27 Mike England; 28–9 John Miller/Garden Picture Library; 31 Philippe Perdereau; 32 Marijke Heuff (Wisley Gardens); 33 Michael Boys/Boys Syndication; 34 Michèle Lamontagne; 35 Marijke Heuff; 36 Tania Midgley; 39 Marijke Heuff (Garden Mien Ruys); 42 Michael Boys/Boys Syndication; 43 Andrew Lawson; 44 Photos Horticultural; 45 Didier Willery/Garden Picture Library; 48 Andrew Lawson; 49 Gary Rogers; 50 Jane Taylor; 51 Michèle Lamontagne; 52 Eric Crichton; 53 above Peter Woloszynski; 53 below Eric Crichton; 54 Photos Horticultural; 55–6 Marijke Heuff (Mr. & Mrs. van der Upwich-Koffer); 58–9 Georges Lévêque; 60 Steven Wooster/Garden Picture Library; 61 Marijke Heuff (Mr. & Mrs. van der Upwich-Koffer); 62 Philippe Perdereau; 63 Tommy Candler/Garden Picture Library; 64 Marijke Heuff (Mrs. L. Kloeg-Amerlaan, Holland); 65 left Elizabeth Whiting and Associates; 65 right Noel Kavanagh; 68 Jacqui Hurst/Boys Syndication; 69 Didier Willery/Garden Picture Library; 70 S & O Mathews; 71 Tania Midgley; 73 S & O Mathews; 76 Rodney Hyett/Elizabeth Whiting and Associates; 77 left Christine Ternynck; 77 right Andrew Lawson; 78 Marijke Heuff; 79 Brian Carter/Garden Picture Library; 82–4 Tania Midgley; 85 Georges Lévêque; 86 Hugh Palmer; 87 left Marijke Heuff (Mr. & Mrs. van der Upwich-Koffer); 87 right S & O Mathews; 88 Jane Taylor; 89 above Tania Midgley; 89 below Marijke Heuff; 90 Photos Horticultural; 91 Eric Crichton; 93 Photos Horticultural; 96 Andrew Lawson; 97 Tania Midgley; 98 Hugh Palmer; 99 Gary Rogers/Garden Picture Library; 100–1 Gary Rogers; 102 Andrew Lawson; 103 Tania Midgley; 104 S & O Mathews; 105 Juliette Wade; 106–7 Tania Midgley; 108 Marijke Heuff; 110–3 Photos Horticultural; 115 Brian Carter/Garden Picture Library; 116 Photos Horticultural; 120 John Elsley; 123 Photos Horticultural.

The publisher also thanks: Vanessa Courtier, Lesley Craig, Tristram Holland, Barbara Nash and Janet Smy, Alistair Plumb and Helen Ridge.